S0-ASK-324

GROWING
SEASONS

Karen,

Happy Planting!

Annie Spiker

GROWING SEASONS

Half-baked Garden Tips, Cheap Advice on Marriage
and Questionable Theories on Motherhood

Annie Spiegelman

SEAL
PRESS

GROWING SEASONS:
HALF-BAKED GARDEN TIPS, CHEAP ADVICE ON MARRIAGE AND
QUESTIONABLE THEORIES ON MOTHERHOOD

© 2003 by Annie Spiegelman

Published by
Seal Press
An Imprint of Avalon Publishing Group Incorporated
1400 65th Street, Suite 250
Emeryville, CA 94608

All rights reserved. No part of this book may be reproduced or transmitted in any form without written permission from the publisher, except by reviewers who may quote brief excerpts in connection with a review.

Library of Congress Cataloging-in-Publication Data is available.

ISBN 1-58005-079-4

9 8 7 6 5 4 3 2

Designed by Paul Paddock
Printed in Canada by Transcontinental
Distributed by Publishers Group West

This one's for you Ma.

Ultimately, we have just one moral duty: to reclaim large areas of peace in ourselves, more and more peace, and to reflect it towards others.

—Etty Hillesum,
*An Interrupted Life: The Diaries
of Etty Hillesum, 1941–43*

TABLE OF CONTENTS

ACKNOWLEDGMENTS

My deepest gratitude to my editor, Ingrid Emerick, for her invaluable skill, enthusiasm, friendship and hard work in bringing this book to print.

Thank you, Roy M. Carlisle, for introducing me to my agent, Kristen Auclair. After two publishing companies with which I was contracted filed for bankruptcy, it was you two who got me off the couch and away from daytime reruns of *Saturday Night Live*.

I am forever grateful to my exceptional midwife, Rosanne Gephart, for placing baby Jack into my arms for the very first time, and to our loving pediatrician, Dr. Bill Liebman, who affectionately cared for Jack in those early years. Bouquets of thanks to the Marin Master Gardener Training Program and to my favorite nursery, Cottage Garden Growers in Petaluma California, for making my garden look like I just may know what I'm doing.

To my six-and-a-half best girlfriends: Far be it from you to stoop so low and count how many times you are mentioned throughout the book. . . . In some very bizarre way you keep my spirit shining bright.

Mushy-gushy love and heaps of gratitude to my sisters, Augusta, Sharon and Carol, for still speaking to me after I write these very personal books about our family.

Big fat hugs to you, Daddy. Thanks for teaching me about love, family, self-determination, European coffee, Godiva chocolates, Dijon mustard, Marx Brothers movies and the IRS.

And then there's Bill. My rock of Gibraltar, my *Spy vs. Spy* true love and some days, when I look especially pitiful, my guest editor. You can bet if there is a clever line or two in this book, he will take credit for it. . . .

GROWING SEASONS

QUEEN BEE GLOSSARY

The following Hebrew and Yiddish terms have been used throughout the manuscript in dialogue by my mother:

Goy-toy: A non-Jewish hunk. (My mother referring to my husband.)

Kishkes: A person's intestines. (*"Tsk-tsk-tsk. She wears shmates just to take my kishkes out."*)

Maspick!: Enough! (*Maspick with the shtuyot!*)

Meshugah: Crazy.

Shmate: Rag. (See "kishkes" above; mix and match.)

Shtuyot: Nonsense. (See "maspick!" above.)

Tchotchkes: Knickknacks.

Tsk-tsk-tsk: Either the end of the world, or someone's sister just slept with her mother's ex-best friend's half-sister's cousin on *Jerry Springer*.

Uch!: Warning, warning. A good clue to exit immediately.

SEPTEMBER 26

"Your People" Barely Survive the First Year

Dear Jack,

The night you were born, the moon burned fire red. It was a balmy autumn night with the last lunar eclipse of the millennium coinciding with a full harvest moon. There was magic in the air. Papa held my hand during each contraction while being forced to listen to, what he later described as, "thirty hours of Bonnie Raitt singing my-man-did-me-wrong songs." Without much sleep Grandma Gin-Gin skillfully managed to photo-document my entire labor. Needless to say, I was not feeling photogenic. Most of the pictures are of me and a sterile-looking hospital clock above my head. As the hours ticked away, I looked more and more miserable. Somewhere during the twentieth hour, and in between contractions, I remember freshening up and putting on some Picture Perfect Pink lipstick. Despite increasing delirium, I sensed a camera was nearby. Your other grandma, the Queen Bee, later remarked she was very proud of me for that and that she had brought me up right.

After thirty-plus hours of labor you made your grand appearance. Roseanne, our midwife, cried when you finally arrived and took your first breath. Papa had tears in his eyes too as he watched your skinny reptilian body pop out. He smiled at me and proclaimed ecstatically, "It's a boy!"

"A boy?" I shuttered. *Are you sure?* What do I know about boys, except that they later turn into men? I come from a family of opinionated, indignant and independent women. We have no patience for boys or men. They are an enigma to us; like unclaimed baggage or understanding your cellular phone service. But once you were in my arms, I was in love and I knew exactly what I had to do.

I would make you the perfect guy.

Vive la femme!

A week or so after your birth, my cackling and ear-splitting family descended upon our tiny calm house. Grandpa, the Queen Bee, Uncle Jim, Cousin Rebecca and my sisters (your aunts Carol, Sha and Augusta). It was just like old times. The Queen Bee yelled at me because you were too skinny and because I should have been resting instead of having all these visitors. Then she went on about your name. "Oy, Dakota, Jack Dakota? How do you spell Dakota? Why does he need so many letters?"

In the middle of this loud and chaotic family gathering in our once peaceful house, you kept me awake every two hours. As I slid wearily into sleep deprivation and postpartum depression, I was surrounded by heated debates about natural childbirth, circumcision and breast-feeding in public. Aunt Augusta decided this was the "picture perfect pink" time to come out.

"Uch, what do you mean, you're a lesbian?" shouted the Queen Bee to no one in particular. "Who did I bring up? Married two times and now she decides to become a lesbian. What is this nonsense? Now she's joining a cult?"

"Ma, it's not a cult," I reassured her, trying to protect my sister and my mother at the same time.

"And why isn't there any Sweet'n Low in this house?" My mother jabbed back at me.

"Because artificial sweeteners cause brain damage in rats," I barked back.

"For this I have to suffer?"

Well, Jack, as you can imagine, all mayhem broke out. Grandpa took you out into the garden so you wouldn't have to hear your first but certainly not last family squabble. I tiptoed out behind him. You slept in Grandpa's lap as he painfully queried me as to whether this was just a stage Augusta was going through. I told him I didn't think so. I admired Augusta's courage to be honest with the family, who I know wants to love her unconditionally even though they may not understand her choices. But I was also concerned for my parents. This was all a bit too much for them.

Moments later the Queen Bee came out to the garden and swiped you right out of your grandpa's arms. I went inside to support Aunt Augusta. As I passed by the sunny kitchen window, I could see my parents who had been divorced for more than twenty years sitting amicably on the deck below the tall red hollyhocks, taking turns kissing you from head to toe.

That was a year ago. Today we are in Idyllwild, California, on a vacation to celebrate your first birthday. It's pouring rain and you woke up at 5:30 A.M. crying for milk. Papa and I fought about who should get up. Then we remembered that we should be nice to you and to each other on this special day. We both got up to play with you and you proceeded to leak through your diaper onto the white hotel carpet. Jack Dakota, this motherhood stuff is rough. Though it looks good on the résumé, I don't think I'm the best candidate for the job. You're too demanding. You need "your people" too much. Papa and I aren't enough. We need help. We need sleep. We need the whole damn village!

Tomorrow we'll drive to San Diego to celebrate your birthday at Aunt Carol's house. I'm a bit perturbed with her. She and I have always been competitive with each other. I admit it. I think all twins are. She skillfully pretends she is not competing with me, but she is actually quite transparent. She is quietly vying for the prize!

I taught her how to garden less than a year ago, and last week she called me, coyly bragging in rapid carefree cadences about her prolific garden and how little she does to make it thrive. She and your uncle Scott have forty perfect tomatoes and five huge, sweet watermelons, their roses are still blooming and their citrus trees (planted by the previous owners) are loaded with fat lemons and limes. I didn't admit to her that my tomato plants all have Verticillium wilt, a soilborne fungus. Even the supposedly disease-resistant ones look really, really pitiful.

It figures she would have healthy plants, make it look easy and be all chipper about it. She is *so* competitive!

Anyway, Happy Birthday, Jack.

"Your people"

OCTOBER

Codependence

Dear Jack,

We just received the pictures from your first birthday party. You look so handsome and I am such a proud mother. There's a wonderful photograph of you sitting on your grandma's lap. You are both laughing. I know it means a lot to the Queen Bee that you feel close to her. On our last day in San Diego, as we were leaving her apartment, you ran out of the elevator and back into her arms, where she was standing in her doorway dressed in her robe waving to you. It brought tears to my eyes. The love I feel for both of you is so extraordinary. Plus, it seems that since you came on the scene, the Queen Bee is nicer to me. I go on about you all the time. This is safe territory. We have found common ground. It makes us both happy. We now have you as a topic instead of all the draining mother-daughter stuff we usually argue about.

Today, however, she slipped back into her usual enigmatic self. She yelled at me for whispering on the phone while you were taking a nap. She later hung up on me because she couldn't hear me.

For every little step we take forward we seem to take one back.

🦋 🦋

Today I received a letter from the Master Gardeners!! They want to interview me.

The Master Gardener program is a training course provided by the University of California Cooperative Extension. Each year they choose thirty-five students out of approximately 150 applicants. Master Gardeners serve as horticultural consultants to home gardeners in the community. They answer public inquiries and provide information on plant health and gardening practices. To be certified a Master Gardener you must complete a sixty-plus-hour training program, pass a final exam and contribute many hours of internship, continuing education and community service within the first year.

I have applied before but have never been chosen (obviously a big mistake on their part). The last time I interviewed, I had just completed a three-month film project. I was exhausted and completely burned out. I could barely stay awake through the interview but still managed to go on and on about how busy I was and how I would try to fit them into *my* schedule. That didn't get me anywhere. Three days later, I received a rejection letter. This time I'm going to get it. I'll say that I have loads of time to volunteer for all their goody-goody projects and will not miss a class. I'll selectively omit the facts that I have a demanding film career, that I am a new mom and that I haven't slept in a year.

Just got off the phone with the Queen Bee, who was in a splendid mood. She had just watched *Martha Stewart Living* on television. "Your friend Martha has such a relaxing voice," she chimed. She had seen a segment we filmed here in the Bay Area about the San Francisco Flower Market. Martha and "her people" were here in

August and I had the chance to work with them. We shot at some of my favorite nurseries and gardens. I was in heaven. The last day of filming was at Rayford Reddell's Garden Valley Ranch in Petaluma, where we filmed him cutting roses for bouquets.

Martha had just purchased a new hi-tech digital camera. Martha, me and Rayford, surrounded by his outstanding rose garden at sunset, posed for photos. Dorky me was so excited to be one of Martha's people that my pudgy face looks like it's about to burst. Of course, that's the picture my mother shows to anyone who's interested, declaring that Martha and her daughter are close personal friends.

After discussing "my friend" Martha, your grandma moved on to you. She loves to hear all the simple things you do. Which is fortunate, as I enjoy talking about you and would probably bore my friends to death. I'm glad she's in good spirits these days. The past few months she has been in and out of the hospital with diabetes-related complications. She drove the hospital staff absolutely crazy. The nurses quickly learned to either agree with her or hide. After her release she had home care but complained that "they're ruining my carpet. All this coming and going. Enough traffic!" So that ended that! Next she phoned her doctor and complained that she was taking too many pills. He changed her medication and now she seems great. She must've intuitively known that she didn't need all those pills.

Her latest theory, at age seventy-two, is that her eye doctor has a crush on her. She swears her fifty-year-old married optometrist is flirting with her. This flirting phenomenon runs in our family. Your papa says I think just about every man who talks to me is flirting with me. Just the other day I came home from work and told him about this cute young actor, who I assume was flirting with me because he was interested in hearing about *me* for five minutes and kept asking more questions about *me*. Papa, looking bored with the same old topic (me), said, "That's nice, Babe."

Okay, maybe he wasn't flirting. Maybe he was just being overly nice to me so I would wrap him early and he could make his audition for a national Nike spot. Just using me! Figures.

He wasn't that cute anyway.

I hope his audition sucks.

This relationship you and I have is so codependent. I thought my relationship with my mother was unbearably confusing. Now I have you and I'm even more perplexed. Each day is filled with such emotional ups and downs. I'm beginning to see why the world is the way it is. As a child your parents make you barely functional, and as a parent your children drive you absolutely insane. Let's just face it. It's virtually impossible to come out normal.

For instance, take last night.

3:00 A.M.
You're hysterically crying.
You are teething.
I give you some Tylenol and tuck you into bed with us.

3:30 A.M.
You are still crying. Your papa walks you around the house.
He changes your diaper and sings goofy songs to you that rhyme with "Chop-Chop" (the nickname he gave you because you are our own little whirling dervish).

4:00 A.M.

You are still in pain, so now I really start to worry.

I feel sorry for you.

I hug you and hold you tight.

I get an upset stomach because I can't bear to have you in pain.

4:30 A.M.

You're still awake. You're quite vocal about it. Maybe a bit too loud.

I walk you around the living room in circles.

Each time I put you into your crib, you cry louder.

This does not go over so well.

I'm so tired and so wide awake at the same time.

I begin plotting my escape at sunrise. I start planning what to put in my suitcase.

I begin writing the farewell note in my head.

I calculate how much breast milk I will need to pump to leave in the freezer for you and Papa.

I imagine how I can run away . . . without looking like a *bad* mother.

I begin to wonder why I ever had a baby in the first place?

Babies *freak me out!*

What could I have been thinking?

I am ready to give you back.

5:00 A.M.

We're sitting in the rocking chair listening to Bonnie Raitt softly sing "Louise."

You fall asleep in my arms wrapped in your fleece blanket.

The early morning sun is just making its way through the living room window.

I stare at you in awe.
Your face is so pure.
I can't believe how much I love you.
Please don't ever leave me.
I can't live without you.

Today the three of us spent the afternoon placing concrete stones around the border of the front yard. We found them at a retirement home that was digging out its driveway and replacing it with a lawn. I went inside to ask the lady at the front desk if we could take pieces of broken concrete from the messy pile near the Dumpster in their driveway. She looked at me as if I were slightly demented and carefully said, "Take as much concrete as you want, miss." I ran out of the lobby practically skipping with excitement. We piled up the jeep with about a hundred concrete rocks and brought them over to our front yard. We spent hours placing rocks. Of course, Papa and I each had our own ideas of how to design them. I decided to go along with his plan because it was actually a better idea. I didn't admit that to him.

Obviously.

Right before sundown we did some light pruning and turned the compost pile. You were busy chasing Maui and Fatcat with your spray bottle, while our neighbor, Bec, practiced her piano really loudly, playing "She'll Be Coming Round the Mountain When She Comes" over and over and over.

Enough with the *mountain!*

Tonight I was busy trying to make your dinner, keep an eye on you and talk to a fancy-pants Hollywood producer on the phone all at the same time. I didn't want her to know that I was a mother because then she'd figure I wasn't available twenty-four/seven and I'd never get the job. She wouldn't stop talking to take a breath. She pushed on, in a rapid-fire, type-A, I-live-for-this-business voice. I don't even have the job yet and Miss Yakkity-Yak told me every single detail of her three-hour production meeting yesterday with the advertising agency. Like I care!! Juggling the phone while I put teriyaki sauce on the chicken, I began wondering where you were and why you were being so quiet. I walked into the living room to find you holding the big spatula from the outdoor grill, chasing poor attention-starved Maui around the house trying to swat her like a fly. I told Miss Yakkity-Yak I really had to go. She seemed a bit perturbed that I had a life.

Now I'm absolutely sure I won't get the job.

I hung up the phone and reprimanded you with a time out. Maui has been so neglected since the day you were born, yet for some reason she still loves us all. She obviously has self-esteem issues. She's afraid we'll give her away, just like we did with our last cat. Max tried to *pretend* he was normal. Once a day he'd come over, all sweet and innocent, to sit in my lap for a few minutes and let me pet him. Just when I thought for a fraction of a moment that I liked him, out of nowhere, for no reason at all, he would bite me, hiss at me, scratch me and fly off my lap as if he'd just seen a ghost, or maybe a dog! I was secretly happy to have an excuse to give him away. When I brought Max back to the humane society, I explained to them that I had a baby who would pull the cat's tail and then the cat would hiss at and attack the baby. The young animal-rights volunteer looked at me like I was insane for returning the cat instead of getting rid of the savage baby.

Today you took a three-hour nap. There is no better gift you can give us. Thank you.

While you napped, Papa and I went into the garden and did some pruning, dividing and fertilizing of the perennials.

Your godparents, Mr. Louie and Pucci, came over in the afternoon. Pucci and I sat in the garden, sipping jasmine tea while we read the newspaper and discussed politics. Papa and Mr. Louie watched three hours of football. After the game they watched the postgame show of the game's highlights. This was followed by further in-depth analysis. Then the two of them critiqued the commentator's analysis of the game for a while before rewinding the videotape to rewatch the game. This madness was finally capped off by their watching an old Super Bowl game from 1985. It was a veritable football triathlon.

You could literally see the brain cells dying off.

I was so repulsed by their behavior that I began viciously searching the Sunday paper for ads of horrific dolls, tacky porcelain plates and goody-goody Thomas Kinkade paintings. This weekend's paper had a particularly good variety: "Rapunzel, Rapunzel, Let Down Your Hair," "John Wayne in a Bubble" and "Jesus Walking on Water."

I filled out all three order forms with Mr. Louie's address. C.O.D.

I feel especially good about myself today.

Yesterday I placed a discolored, aged clay pot on the back bench. I spent a long time deciding its correct placement in the garden. I was trying to see if it worked there, if it could be called "art." Papa came home an hour later. From the kitchen window I watched him entering the backyard, ready to bet a million dollars he would absolutely hate it. He immediately picked up the old vase, along with some garden tools on the grass, and tossed it into the shed.

I yelled out the window to him, "Babe, that's art!"

He put it back, stared at it, shook his head, then stared at me and walked away.

Sometimes I wonder how we've lasted this long.

English Lavender
Botanical name: *Lavandula angustifolia*
Family: Labiatae
"Whaaa-whaa" rating: 2

This is an easy, sun-loving perennial that blooms spring to fall with fragrant foliage and little care. Grows 3-4 feet tall with gray scented leaves and clusters of small purple flowers on long spikes. Good border plants that require little water or fertilizer.

Universal botanical "whaaa-whaa" rating system:
Blooms and asks little of the gardener: 1
Hungry, thirsty, needy and cranky: 10

NOVEMBER

Bribery and the Master Gardener Interview

Dear Jack,

Just got back from the Master Gardener interview! Dressed in full floral skirt and sunflower yellow shirt, I looked like a mix between a Barbie doll and a walking ad for the gardening store Smith & Hawken. At the last minute, thinking it was all a bit too much, I ditched the straw hat with the ugly plastic roses on the brim and threw on my NY Yankees hat backward. As I left the driveway, I rubbed my hands in a scented geranium plant so I would look and smell botanical.

When I walked into the boardroom, one of the interviewers began to sneeze and cough as if she was having a bad allergic reaction to scented geranium. I pretended not to notice. I just went on talking about myself and how I love, Love, *Love* to give back to the community. I told them how I enjoy interacting with other gardeners, how helpful I could be working at the Master Gardener desk and how happy it would make me to answer questions from other gardeners. Like I care about their gardens. . . .

(I didn't say that.)

I bragged about you for a while. I told them how much you help me in the garden and went on and on about how smart and advanced you are. I sensed the interviewers were getting bored, so

I quickly changed the subject to your papa. I admitted to them that I wanted to know more about gardening than my husband and how that would give me great pleasure. Because they were all women, we instantly bonded. Everyone began exchanging information about their partners or ex-partners. Vive la femme! This little session of sisterhood therapy went on for a few minutes and then the interview was over. I forgot to mention my desire to get my very own Master Gardener pin! On my way out I gave them a signed copy of my last book and skillfully insinuated that they should accept me into the program so they could be part of my next book.

At the time I really had no plans to write another book.

Is that bribery?

Yesterday, after a teary farewell to you, our neighbor Betty and I drove off. We ran away from our lives for thirty-six hours and you did great alone with your wonderful papa. We went up to Indian Springs in Calistoga to get some well-deserved pampering. We had massages and mud baths and drank pints of cucumber-orange water. It was such a peaceful day. I thought of you often but I knew I needed to get away so I could get some rest.

Not that you're exhausting or demanding or anything like that . . .

Last night when I was ready to go to sleep, Betty literally forced me to put my bathing suit on and go for a night swim with her. We swam in a heated Olympic-size pool all by ourselves. There was steam rising above the water, which made it look foggy and mysterious. It felt like a dream, just Betty and me in this huge pool, fluttering around on neon-colored Styrofoam floats, telling stories. I watched her swimming around looking so carefree. For a moment she reminded me of her daughter Bec, so sweet and inno-cent. It seems like a higher power decided that we should live right next door to each other. How lucky is that to have been handed a neighbor and a best friend all in one package—one of the really great gifts in my life. The very next gift was the fact that I got to sleep for ten hours straight that night and woke up to birds' chirping and no immediate place to be or thing to do for anyone else but *me*.

Imagine that!

The next morning there were more gifts to come. While sipping coffee in a Calistoga café, to our surprise, in walked my good friends and extended family Barbara and Wendy. Wendy is my les-bian Martha Stewart, a most gracious hostess who greets me at her San Francisco Victorian door wearing red lipstick and hip Euro-pean black shoes and hands me a cocktail and an exquisite canapé hors d'oeuvre, as I arrive tired and cranky after a long day on the set. Barbara should simply be elected "The Lesbian Ambassador." Within five minutes of meeting her, you are proudly wearing purple and waving the rainbow flag.

After more speedy coffee the four of us went back to Indian Springs to swim in the pool. We kicked around on floats and dis-cussed politics, work, babies, music and straight and gay relation-ships. I was doing my usual rambling on about *men* when Barbara stopped me midsentence and said, "You know, Annie, get over it. Wendy and I have challenges too. Lesbian relationships are no easier than heterosexual ones."

What a *bummer*. I thought *men* were the problem.

Grandpa is visiting from New York City. I don't know who gets more excited for his visits, you or me. Your papa, you, me and Grandpa went out to Sunday brunch. At the restaurant you stuffed your little face and picked at everyone's plates with your grimy hands. When you were done, you wandered outside onto the deck. There, you promptly found wet leaves, old french fries and whatever else you could cram into your mouth before I could catch you. I tried to bring you back to the table but you started crying. The whole restaurant stared at me as if I should do something to make you stop. The three of us took turns watching you on the deck while the others finished eating. My poor dad has now become one of "your people" too.

Later that evening Grandpa took care of you while Papa and I went out. Freedom! We played Van Morrison and Etta James in the car, singing and laughing because we were *free!*

Yippee! We went to the local bookstore. I found a half-dozen books in women's literature, while your papa spent at least an hour in the sports section and then went to the sports section of the magazine rack. When we returned home, Grandpa said he had forgotten how exhausting it is to be around babies, and he credited my mother for working so hard when my sisters and I were young. He had helped when he was home, but he worked most days and often traveled on long business trips. The Queen Bee was left alone with the four of us to do the unpaid work—cooking, cleaning, shopping, chauffeuring, scheduling—work that a fifties mother was expected to perform quietly and happily. She wasn't happy and she wasn't quiet about it. My mother disagreed with the division of labor and my sisters and I often endured her heated and hostile "It's a man's world" rant. Although she achieved impeccable homemaking skills over the years, she didn't arrive there gracefully. She was like Betty Crocker in need of an anger-management class. Tomorrow I may call her and let her know her ex-husband has acknowledged his appreciation of her hard work. Maybe she'll even have something nice to say back.

But I doubt it.

My three favorite directors (not that you asked): Greg Winter, Tom Dusenbery and Randy Field (and I'm not just saying this to get work). (Although that isn't a bad idea.) *Note: Send free copies of book to the above.*

Why are they my favorites? I'm glad you asked. Because on the set we laugh and laugh and laugh. Not at other people's expense, well, maybe sometimes, maybe a sound guy or two, but usually we are making fun of ourselves and what wrong turn we made in our pathetic movie careers that led us here, in a ticky-tacky supermarket at 3:00 A.M. in Pacifica, lighting the meat freezer. And taking it very, very seriously. Discussing the placement of the chopped chuck, the boneless rolled rump roast and the pork butt roast. Should the rolled rump roast be facing front or back, up or down, in or out? We discuss this and much worse with the clients and the ad agency art director who is looking through the camera commenting on the scanty lighting and why the leg of lamb is in the shadow. Is this normal conversation to be having? Shouldn't we be discussing world peace or famine and how all this meat that we are putting under hot lights will be ruined and wasted? And I'm thinking how can we cook it and feed it to the homeless before it starts smelling, and then it is 5:00 A.M. and we are still discussing meat products and packaging and should the pull dates show and should we bring in the chopped sirloin—who forgot the sirloin? Heads are rolling, meat is stinking, the generator just died . . . *stop!!*

Can they not see that we are *artists*? And writers and poets and revolutionaries and creators of aesthetic photographic genius. Can they not see that we have sold our souls and that we know it and we feel sick to our stomachs about it? Can they not see how we crave to be back in the darkroom developing our black and white photographs and discussing artsy things like foreign cinema, dark literature, anarchistic political uprisings and precious gems?

Precious gems?

Precious gems. That's something Randy would say on the set, in between takes and imitations of his father's Yiddish accent, and the crew would immediately stop gorging at the Craft Service table and momentarily pay attention, only because he was telling another one of his funny family stories. Then we'd resume filming and the crew would resume eating and whispering their long stories at the Craft Service table. Or is it the way Greg wore the round, bright yellow baby duck float on his head and continued having abstract conversations about the shot with the client when we were filming at that pool in Santa Rosa? They just stood there shaking their heads agreeing with him. Or is it the way Tom proudly stands on the set, on top of an apple box and announces "Strive for mediocrity" that makes the crew want to achieve the impossible for him.

Are these men good role models?

Some may think not.

Spoke to Ma early this morning. The Queen Bee is still very disappointed that we will not be with her this Thanksgiving. I will miss her too. I miss the "girls-only" Thanksgivings I spent with my mom and sisters back when we were all single. My mother, having been kept out of school to help support her destitute family, always stressed education, and my dad coached us each from a young age into aggressively climbing the ladder of our chosen field. It worked. We are now successful independent women who have each purchased our own home or business. But when we come within five feet of our mother, we are reduced to fifteen-year-old snippy, rebellious preteens. In between rolling our eyes at our mother's wise yet redundant comments, we secretly want her to smother us with her warm hugs and kisses. All of a sudden we are needy and confused.

Aunt Augusta was a professor at the University of Dallas, Texas. We'd spend the holiday loafing around her house, eating turkey sandwiches and playing Pictionary till midnight with our mother, who would always win. She was the only one of us that could draw. The day after Thanksgiving we'd sit at the kitchen table and she'd try so patiently to teach me how to paint a fruit bowl, her specialty. But my fruit bowl always came out lopsided and pitiful looking. She would cheer me on and tell me how beautiful I was drawing but then, when she couldn't hold it in a second longer, we'd both crack up, laughing at my painfully pathetic attempt at fruit art. Sometimes we laughed so hard we'd have tears in our eyes. My mother would say it's time for a break and we'd make coffee.

It was late November and below freezing but the Queen Bee needed her daily allotment of fresh air, so we'd bundle up in sweaters and wool blankets, grab our coffee cups and sit out in Aunt Augusta's sunny rose garden. Aunt Sha and Aunt Carol would not partake, mostly because they said "we looked insane." Aunt Augusta would be busy fixing up her home and putting little knickknacks, soap, clean wash cloths and surprise paper-backs on each of our guest beds. Aunt Carol would get some out-dated book on medicine, Aunt Sha would get *People* magazine and I'd get either *Guerrilla Feminism, Codependent No More* or *Surrender the Pink.*

Along with my copy of *Codependent No More* and a nice hot cup of coffee, I'd shuffle out the frozen sliding door and sit with my mom for as long as I could take the cold and the unpredictable repartee. The conversation would dip and turn, but somehow we'd always go back to my mother's agonizing childhood. I don't know if she just needed to talk about it again, or if I just needed to analyze it again.

Her parents had abandoned her around the age of four in a wretched orphanage in Russia. Her father told her he'd be back in the morning and showed up three years later. After her parents had a few more children, they came to take my mother back to their new home in Haifa, Israel. They kept her out of school to help at the family barbershop where my grandfather reigned. Over the years she ran away from home frequently, but he would find her, bring her back and beat her. At seventeen she had finally saved enough money to travel to France, where she found a job as a nanny and later made her way to the States. She praised America and had found her new home in, as she calls it, the center of the universe: New York City. When all of us grew up and moved out, my mother finally got her own education by attending high school and college, graduating from Marymount College at age fifty-nine to a standing ovation.

Just when I am feeling so much love and compassion for her, understanding her anger toward real and imaginary villains, seeing her as the true brave heroine she is and wanting to hug and slobber her with kisses, *the slope gets slippery.* She yells at me for not bringing out enough packages of Sweet'n Low. It is definitely time to get out of the cold.

Jack, you fell asleep in my arms tonight at seven o'clock. You were warm and cuddly and I was so in love with you, especially because you went to bed early. After tiptoeing into your bedroom, avoiding the squeaky floorboard and putting you carefully into your crib, Papa and I did our "he's asleep" high-five celebratory ritualistic dance around the living room. Then we took a nature walk around the garden. A hard rain was falling, but that didn't stop us from doing a full-fledged tour of Papa's newly planted Shasta daisy seedlings! The rain soon turned into a drizzle, so we decided to prune a few overgrown plants and deadhead some others. We cut back the overgrown princess flower near the kitchen window. Papa went inside to direct the pruning while I did the cutting. I could barely hear him over the sound of the rain, but I nodded to him as if I could and just continued to happily prune the plant the way I felt like doing it. He knows me too well, though. He knew I couldn't hear him so he began gesturing like a madman and pulling up his pants to remind me just who wears the pants in the house.

I'm glad you weren't awake to witness that.

Survived another Thanksgiving without slitting my wrists. I try to not be so jaded and full of angst at this time of year only because Papa has such good childhood memories of the Christmas season. I have good holiday memories too, but I have problems with the overcommercialization, the constant Christmas music blaring out of sidewalk speakers and the Thomas Kinkade porcelain Nativity figurines in gift shop windows I pass on the way to work. It all puts me on the verge of hiding alone in my room listening to old Neil Young albums and devouring a pint of Ben & Jerry's Chunky Monkey.

Papa says I'd feel less guilty if I'd just go for the wrists.

Thanksgiving was at Grandma Gin-Gin's. You got to play with your cousins Casey, Gary, Ryan, Stefan and Taylor. Grandma Gin-Gin has begun keeping tabs on which daughter- or son-in-law shows up for each occasion at her home. This may be a new tactic or maybe she has secretly been doing it for years without us knowing. She goes around snapping photos of all the guests, and when we have all departed, she meticulously documents in her diary the year, the occasion and exactly who was in attendance. I recently discovered this as I was quietly sitting in the den below the Thomas Kinkade wall tapestry, eating my second piece of pumpkin pie and about to pass out. I witnessed a heated discussion between Papa's sister Mammer-Jammer, her husband Skeeter and Grandma Gin-Gin.

Mammer and Skeeter were adamantly arguing that they had been at this very house two Thanksgivings ago and *not* at Skeeter's parent's home. With a sly smile on her face Grandma Gin-Gin pulled out her photo albums and her diary from two years ago to prove to them that they were indeed not present. The whole discussion was a bit disturbing but fun to watch! No one wants to get on the matriarch's bad side. She is a very devout woman who attends church regularly and no one doubts her mystical powers. I knew well enough not to get involved, so I just sat there laughing at Skeeter. Ha-ha! He was losing. Tee-hee!

Next was a little game Papa's family plays on holiday occasions where all the guests pick a number and whoever is chosen wins the table centerpiece, which this year was a nice burnt-brown ceramic turkey hand basket with a wide hole in the back to place I'm not sure what. Grandma Gin-Gin wouldn't let me or Papa play. She said Papa and I were banned from the game because in the past we have made fun of the process and the prizes. What a meanie! Just because we'd fall on the floor laughing at the winning prize and label the winner "a loser" shouldn't disqualify us from playing the game. Right? The prizes are tchotchkes! You gotta laugh at tchotchkes!

Grandma Gin-Gin wasn't laughing, however. She just looked at me while shaking her head.

Papa's older brother, Shoobie—a former U.S. National skier who has spent years in India with Mother Theresa saving the poor, homeless lepers and then worked as an emergency room doctor in downtown L.A. and is now studying to become a priest—was staring at me too. Heads turned, eyes squinting. Looking at me as if they knew that the few times my mother and I were invited to a church service, in between the kneeling and the crossing, the crossing and the kneeling, the Queen Bee would be running commentary, and I'd be sitting in the squeaky pew next to her in tears from laughing so hard. "Uch, Annie, *maspick!* Up down, up down. Enough with the *shtuyot*. Is he ever going to stop talking? Uch, now back to Jesus. Leave him alone. The poor guy is dead. More up and down. Uch, my knees!"

The priest and his mother see right through me.

I am going straight to hell in a burnt-brown hand basket.

The three of us have come down with bad colds. You've been very uncomfortable, coughing and teething. Because we're "your people," if you're miserable, we're miserable. At dinner you turned over your plate of leftovers on your head, thinking it was funny. It was your only smile all day. Mine was sharpening a pencil. It was the one undertaking today about which I felt a sense of completion. This is surely a sign of some syndrome or psychosis.

It's been raining the past few days. Every night you and I go into the garden, turn on the Martha Stewart perfect little white Christmas lights and watch the rain. You have on this great red fleece outfit and your black rubber boots. You look like a little elf who shops at the Gap. Tonight we made a bouquet of lavender, Mexican sage and rosemary for your papa, who has taken such good care of us the past few days. Last night he made me tea and brought me gardening magazines and let me sleep with his water pillow. I actually hate his water pillow because it swishes and swashes all night until you're seasick. But he put it under my head and said "smooth sailing" with such love in his eyes that I felt honored to sleep with his special weird pillow. Then, when you woke up coughing and crying at 3:00 A.M., he held you until you fell asleep in his arms. Since you and I have not one iota of patience, we are so very blessed to have someone so kind and patient around us.

PS Mr. Louie received his first gift in the mail: a picture of Ronald Reagan riding a white stallion embossed on a porcelain plate. They charged him fifty bucks plus shipping and handling. He left me an irate accusatory message.

Isn't life grand!!

Well, you can start calling me Master Gardener! I just got the letter saying I've been accepted into the program. The classes start in

January and go for four months. Somehow I'll juggle work, you, Papa and the garden to make the Thursday lectures. I hope you will be understanding and helpful. But I doubt it.

Papa is obsessed with Shasta daisies. Today he planted two more six-packs. He says they're easy and cheerful. How sweet. For a moment I thought I sensed a bit of optimism in his voice and I got worried that he wasn't well. Then he began questioning whether these Shasta daisies were the tall ones that would stand up straight or if they would require staking. Next he claimed the lady at the nursery with all those crystals around her head intentionally ripped him off and sold him the inferior genus. Then he doubted they would bloom at all.

That's when I knew he was just fine.

Mexican Bush Sage

Botanical name: *Salvia leucantha*
Family: Lamiaceae
"Whaaa-whaa" rating: 1

This is a graceful, arching perennial with grayish-green foliage and spikes of purple velvety blossoms. Stalks can be cut down to the ground after the spring flowering and will bloom again in the fall. Grows three to five feet around. Likes full sun and little water.

DECEMBER

Enough with the Christmas Music!

Dear Jack,

Each morning I look forward to hearing your little chirpy voice calling "Mama?" This morning after breakfast we bundled up in layers of fleece and went out to strip the leaves off the rosebushes in preparation for pruning them later this month. You mostly got in my way and distracted me by pretending you were going to run into the street. I would jump up in a panic to save you, rub against a prickly rosebush and scream in pain. Just then you'd change your mind and stop right before the end of the driveway.

PS I'm beginning to accept the fact that the Christmas music and sleigh bells ringing in my head may never go away.

Just got an invitation to a reunion party from Stuffy. Let me tell you about Stuffy. Stuffy was our birthing instructor. Back when I was pregnant with you, Papa and I were absolutely clueless about the actual delivery of a baby. Because we were both in very, very deep-seated denial that you were ever going to be a real living thing, we thought it might be a good idea to take some birthing classes.

The classes were once a week for eight weeks. Because of work and our lack of interest, we missed a few of them. In fact, even after going to half of the classes, we'd still manage to get lost on the way there and then rationalize that it was better to go out for ice cream than to walk into Stuffy's class late. One week Stuffy gave us dirty looks and told us our attendance record was not good. We suspected she didn't like us because we sat in the back row, took little naps while she talked, looked bored, snickered a lot and always tried to sneak out early.

Her classes were full of good information and she was very knowledgeable, but she had this bad habit of finishing her sentences with "and stuff." To stay interested, I would count how many times she said "and stuff." To keep your papa awake, I would kick him each time she did it. She usually averaged sixteen times an hour. So Papa decided to call her "Stuffy." After a while, we forgot what her real name was and just fondly thought of her as Stuffy. Stuffy's class, Stuffy's notes, Stuffy's stuff and Stuffy's reunion party that we will not be attending because we had no friends in the class because our classmates were all a little too perky and happy about having babies.

Imagine that?!

Sometimes, though, I did actually pay attention in Stuffy's class, especially when we were learning breathing techniques for pain during labor. But your papa was very, very bad. If he wasn't catnapping, he was reading the sports page, which he had carefully disguised in between the birthing pamphlets or had hidden under his jacket. Or he'd be busy whispering very negative things to me about "Bubbles" and "Precious," the goody-goody male classmates who sat in the front row hugging their pregnant partners, asking relevant questions and being genuinely supportive of the mothers of their soon-to-be-babies.

Imagine that?!

✄ ✄

The three of us just got back from a long trip to Southern California, the site of another family lovefest. We went to visit the Queen Bee in San Diego and to celebrate Cousin Rebecca's second birthday. The third morning in San Diego, Augusta, her partner, Deb, Uncle Jim and Aunt Sha went out to breakfast while I watched you and Cousin Rebecca. There had apparently been some heated political debate between Uncle Jim and Aunt Augusta during the breakfast. Aunt Augusta didn't appreciate his philosophical comments, which she perceived as being close-minded, so she attacked him in her big bad-ass-karate-black-belt-feminist-Ph.D. tone! Then breakfast was officially over. Now, if you ask Aunt Sha, who was stuck between her sister and her husband, she says that the talk at the table was not antagonistic and that Jim was simply making conversation. But if you ask Aunt Augusta or Deb, you get an entirely different picture.

After breakfast the four of them came bursting into Aunt Carol's house where she, Grandpa and I were washing the breakfast dishes, preparing lunch and discussing what we'd be eating for dinner. None of the others were speaking to each other and there was definitely weight in the air.

What a perfect time for the Queen Bee to chime in with her glorious commentary! "Why are they so quiet and why can't she wear some lipstick? Would it kill her to wear some makeup??? And why are they dressed the same? Like a cult!" she not-so-graciously asked anyone who would dare answer. No one answered.

My mother . . . subtle as a rocket launch.

Aunt Augusta said she was fed up with being attacked by her own family and would not be visiting again. "Deb and I have been insulted and we're leaving."

So Deb, without saying a word to any of us, left and sat in the rental car for the next hour, parked across the street. Aunt Augusta passed through the kitchen to pack her bags, when Carol, who was furiously washing the dishes and shouting at her at the same time and speed, stopped her. Every single accusation ended with a plate or serving spoon banging loudly on the dish rack. There she was, clinking pots and pans, waving her soapy hands, as she lamented, "You know what, Augusta? I'm not going to be made to feel guilty all my life because I missed your commitment ceremony. You planned it three weeks after my own wedding. That was brilliant! Hmmmm, let's see, should I go to Hawaii on my honeymoon or, should I go to the boondocks of Illinois to hang out with a bunch of lesbian feminists?"

I still feel guilty because I didn't make it to her commitment ceremony, but it was really bad timing. There isn't a good enough excuse not to be there. But at the time you were nine months old and I wasn't ready to leave you, nor was I ready to travel long distances with you. At that point in your life it was unbearable to be with you on a plane for too long. You could sit still for only twenty minutes. After that you demanded that "your people" keep walking you up and down the aisle or let you crawl around the plane. If, God forbid, you had to sit still at takeoff and landing, the entire plane heard about it. So Papa and I barely left the house. Let alone the neighborhood. In fact, we didn't leave our zip code. We were two losers and a lump.

I don't ever again want to hear about those people who say they traveled to China when their babies were less than a year old. They're either (a) big, fat liars, (b) giving drugs to their children, or (c) doing really good drugs themselves.

I tried to escape Carol's kitchen dissertation by going out to the patio. The Queen Bee, one of the loudest profanity-droppers I know on the planet, was sitting quietly, gracefully sipping her iced tea with lemon and half a pound of Sweet'n Low. With her hands covering her ears and her eyes squinted, she looked at me and said, "Uch, where did she learn to talk like this? And such language!"

I had to wake you up from your nap and pack all of our bags in about ten minutes. Because the original plan was that you and I would travel to Los Angeles in Augusta's rental car, we were forced to leave a day early because of this emotional upheaval that you so brilliantly slept through. I kissed the Queen Bee good-bye and hugged Grandpa, who was out at the car trying to convince Deb to come back in.

So the four of us drove away from the house with Carol waving her dishrag, still adamantly going on about how *right* she was, and the Queen Bee mumbling, "Uch, what's the big deal? She shouldn't take it so seriously. So what if her parents are square? Gay, shmay. Enough with this nonsense! Let them go. And where's the cheesecake? Now we can have the whole cake to ourselves. I'll have some coffee!"

We drove for an hour mostly in silence. Then you chimed in, crying for the entire second hour because you didn't want to sit in your car seat. What is it you have against sitting still? I sat in the back with you, trying to pretend I didn't know you, just imagining what the two Ph.D.'s in the front were thinking about me and my loud kid. I was worrying about the family, about you and about the job I was beginning the following day in Los Angeles. We were desperate to shut you up, so Deb pulled off the road in Nowheresville. The sign at the exit said "Road 9, Avenue 22 and 1/2." *What? Did they run out names for their streets?* What was more pathetic was the billboard on the side of Road 9 that read: "Next exit Thomas Kinkade Gallery."

He really *is* everywhere.

The only place in sight was a bowling alley. We went in, washed up, had a soda and debated leaving you there with bowling aliens so we could have some peace in the car. The break did us good. You seemed calmer, and we all began to talk a little and even cracked a few jokes. Well, actually, I was the only one laughing. I asked Aunt Augusta, "Do you think Ma really thinks you've joined a lesbian cult?" I just howled with laughter. No one else found it funny.

And then you started crying again.

The commercial I worked on in Los Angeles turned out to be really fun. It is rare, it seems, to have good things to say about the movie business. Papa says I spend my unemployed days looking for work, then get stressed out and depressed because there is no work. And then, when a job finally does come along, I am drained and angry because I have spent fourteen-hour days surrounded by egomaniacs, assassins, opportunists and phonies, and then I just can't wait till the shoot is over.

Wow . . . I must be so pleasant to be around.

On the last day of the shoot we wrapped early and I got to spend a couple of hours with Aunt Augusta before she and Deb were to fly back to Alabama and begin teaching at the university again. Deb babysat for you while Aunt Augusta and I went to the yuppie supermarket that had a coffee stand and two velvet couches. She is the oldest and I am the youngest but we have somehow always remained close. She remembers Carol and me as babies and how she helped change our diapers. I remember her as a teenager when I was in grade school, thinking she was so cool because she used Dippity-do in her hair.

If we are not discussing the Queen Bee and different therapies or names of possible disorders that she may have or ways to get through life *alive* with our mother, then we are discussing only two other topics: gardening and politics. Luckily we agree on both. We discuss rose pruning techniques for a short while, but invariably the conversation winds its way to politics. We sip our coffees and look through the morning paper. There is an article about domestic abuse with alarming statistics. In America a woman is battered by her partner every twelve to fifteen seconds. Eight to ten women lose their lives each day as a result of domestic violence. We read the article together. I get depressed but Augusta becomes proactive. She tells me how she volunteers at a home for abused women in Huntsville. She tells me details about the beds, the stuffed animals and the baby blankets they have set up for these women's children who have to run away in the middle of the night to escape. She tells me there are wealthy battered women and there are poor ones, but they all share the fear they live with. They are traumatized and sometimes barely alive when they come in the door at odd hours.

I watch Augusta's face, hear the power in her voice and see her conviction, and I remember why I love her so much. She is part of the solution, not like the ones who sit around complaining as they watch soap operas, football or the next useless moronic reality show on FOX. She is helping. She is teaching. She is saving someone's daughter or sister or mother. She is amazing.

We've had a rough few days, mostly because you've become what we call on the set HM—high maintenance. It's like we are living with a prima donna rockstar about to slash the hotel room to pieces if he doesn't get what he wants *now!* Today, one minute you're walking around with your filthy, bald, scary baby doll in your arms, sweet-talking to your stuffed animals, and the next you're throwing that scary doll around the living room crying hysterically and walking in circles. I think your teeth are bothering you, or maybe you're just doing what you're supposed to be doing at this age. I don't know. Nothing we could do today made you happy. "Your people" disappointed you. I don't think we'll be invited on your next tour. I wouldn't be surprised if there are pink slips on our desks tomorrow morning.

Your papa and I are trying so hard to be patient with you, which is extremely difficult since you've become possessed. Papa tried to entertain you this morning while I got some rest. In the afternoon, during your naptime, Papa fell asleep on the couch. He was trying to get you to take a nap but, of course, you were wide awake. I know for certain that you stayed awake simply because you didn't want to miss a moment of torturing me. After almost two hours of me begging, threatening and trying to bribe you to take a nap, I put you into the backpack and took you for a walk. It was a beautiful and quiet winter day with holiday spirit in the air. It was so pleasant out and you fell asleep so quickly that I even felt joyful about the holidays for a moment or two.

We took a long walk to the nursery, where I treated myself to a David Austin bare-root rose called Evelyn, an old-fashioned scented apricot rose. On the walk back home the sun was beginning to set and the downtown Christmas lights were lighting up the streets. It was so delightful I almost wanted to wake you up to share it with you, but I quickly came to my senses and let you sleep. When we got home, I somehow managed to get you out of the backpack and onto the couch next to Papa without waking you. You have no idea what an accomplishment that is.

I sneaked my new rose out into the garden without Papa

waking. He thinks I'm obsessed with roses. Then every spring, when the forty-some roses are in glorious full bloom, I hear him chit-chatting across the fence to the admiring neighbors, gladly accepting all the credit, as if he had anything to do with it!!

I turned on the backyard Christmas lights and planted into the cool evening. I was having a wonderful time all by myself when our teamster neighbor, New York Mike, pounded on the backyard gate. He yelled at me because we have only white Martha Stewart lights and no colorful holiday lights on our house. He said I was a !@#$! snob and threatened next year to decorate our house with tacky Santas, gnomes, reindeers and maybe even a baby Jesus, "since after all he was a Jew." Every December the entire neighborhood is forced to listen to Mike's greatest hits of Christmas music, which he plays through a speaker in his backyard, as he yanks out his rosebushes with a rope tied to the back of his truck and replants them in a sunnier location. *(Note: Don't try this at home.)* As he was leaving, I yelled down the driveway, "And another thing, enough with the Christmas music!"

Two minutes later, blasting over the fence, I heard "Do You Hear What I Hear?" sung by what sounded like a Gomer Pyle and Petula Clark duet.

Papa swears it was The Captain and Tennille.

And then, "Whaaaaa."

You were done with your nap.

Shazamm, Shazamm, Shazamm!

This morning I phoned a director whom I haven't seen in over a year about a project we will be working on next month. He wasn't home but his wife answered the phone. They have two small children. She has never met you but was excited to hear all about you and about how I'm enjoying motherhood. I was going on about how I cannot talk on the phone anymore without you interrupting or running around and getting into trouble. And how I can't take my eyes off of you for a second, let alone hold a conversation.

She said, "Yes, I know what you mean," in a high-pitched, squeaky, chipper voice. *"But don't ya just love it?!"*

I was so surprised by her nauseating eager-beaverness that I almost hung up on her. I wanted to say, "No, I *don't* just *love* it! What I love is having a sense of accomplishment, a sense of a beginning and an end to a project or two throughout my day. What I love is having a moment to have one single thought instead of twenty worrisome ones stampeding loudly through my brain at any given time. What I love is not being in cleaning, cooking, shopping, serving and crying-baby crisis mode all day long. What I would really love is for you to come pick up my baby so I can go take a nap."

By this point you were tipping over the kitchen garbage looking for your Super ball so I said I had to go. Is it me? Is something wrong with me that I like an iota of sanity in my home?

As I ponder this, I am trying to make dinner and you are on the kitchen floor throwing a tantrum because I won't give you the butcher knife to play with.

Don't ya just love it!!

New Year's resolution: Stop being judgmental.

Yes, Jack, I've decided that I will make a concerted effort to stop judging people. Withholding judgment is going to be hard, almost impossible really on a film set, but well worth the effort. Maybe I'll have nothing to say about anybody if I can't make a judgment about them. Maybe I'll just become quiet.

This is a good goal.

I hope it works better than last year's resolution to stop eating sugar. That was simply self-sabotage. You were only a few months old and I was feeling very, very overwhelmed. It's totally impossible to expect to achieve too much during those first few months of motherhood. (This is another thing everyone forgot to tell me about having a baby.) If you make it out of your pajamas and into the shower by 10:00 A.M., that's a good day. With you, it was really hard to shower because you'd be crying and wanting "your people" not only to hold you every minute but also to walk you around. We were never allowed to stop moving.

Not that I'm judging you.

Christmas Rose

Botanical name: *Helleborus*
Family: Ranunculaceae
"Whaaa-whaa " rating: 2

Blooms are long-lasting and it is a hardy plant. Its seeds are spread by snails! They eat the oil covering the seeds and carry the rest away in their slime. Likes shade to part shade. Grows about two feet high with white-greenish blossoms. Good cut flowers. Dip stem of cut end in boiling water and then in deep, cold water. This is a magical Christmas time bloomer that even makes a believer out of me.

JANUARY

Seeds

Dear Jack,

We just returned from the coastal town of Bolinas, where we spent a memorable New Year's Eve weekend with your godparents, Mr. Louie and Pucci, and our extended family, Ron and Naomi. You surprised us by being so well behaved. Or maybe it only seemed that way because there were six adults there to take care of your needs. That's just about enough to have a smooth day. The house we stayed in had a beautiful old garden and a sunroom with a stone fireplace. We spent a lot of time there eating and talking and watching you run around the garden.

On New Year's Day you woke "your people" at 6:00 A.M. We bundled you up in layers of yuppie fleece, stuffed you into the backpack and went for a long walk on the beach. You ran around on the sand with your new black hat, looking like a dreamy little water creature that couldn't stop moving or he'd drown.

At night the three of us slept in a king-size bed with an electric blanket. I took a great photograph of you sleeping with Papa. You were luxuriously stretched out across this enormous bed, while your poor papa was curled up and stuffed into a little corner—that about says it all.

On our last night there was an electrical storm. The power went out just as we were preparing to sit down and eat Mr. Louie's legendary lemon and garlic grilled chicken. You fell asleep early and we ended up having a candlelight dinner while Mr. Louie told ghost stories. He told of an encounter he and Papa had twenty-five years ago on a rock climbing trip. They were on a dark logging road on the outskirts of Jackson Hole, Wyoming. He swears there was a parked car in the middle of the road with a female driver whose head spun around 360 degrees and the empty passenger seat kept rocking back and forth. Mr. Louie had me so scared that I kept going into our bedroom every few minutes to make sure the ghosts hadn't carried you away. As the lightning flashed and lit up the ink black night, I tucked you under the covers tightly the way the Queen Bee used to tuck me in. She'd kiss our little foreheads, pat our backs and whisper, "I love you, Mouse. Sleep tight."

Today you are back at Pat's house after she took a well-deserved week off from her daycare for the holidays. I was worried you'd have a hard time going back after spending so much time at home, but you ran through her door without even saying good-bye to me. I think back to a year ago, when I was just returning to work, I would drop you off and you'd be just fine and I'd stumble to the car in tears.

When I got home there was a message from my mom on the answering machine. It went something like this, "Mouse? Mouse, where are you? You're missing the Rockettes on TV. Where could she be at ten in the morning? Why is she never home? It's your mother." Click. By the time I called her back she was out, so I left her a message. I am sure to get in trouble with her later for calling her when she was out.

I started pruning the roses and thinking about the Queen Bee and how she took my sisters and me to see the Rockettes every year at Radio City Hall. We'd get dressed up in our pink wool coats with fancy fake fur collars and white pompom hats. We were each allowed our own box of Milk Duds at the concession counter. For once I didn't have to share with Carol, and that was a really, really big deal. Then we'd spend the rest of the day ice skating at Wollman's Rink in Central Park. My father would take Super 8 movies of my mother trying to hold Carol and me up at the same time. Like an old cartoon, we'd be crashing into the side wall and each other—sometimes crying, sometimes laughing. My mother, dressed in her tight black ski outfit with a rose-colored kerchief around her head and wearing deep-red lipstick, skated smoothly around the obstacle course of fallen daughters, somehow managing to look glamorous as she picked us up one by one and warmed our frozen little hands in hers.

Skating memories had me in a trance and I butchered the poor "Honey Bouquet" rosebush. Luckily, Betty stopped by and inter-rupted me. She asked if I would prune her roses too. I can't believe she trusts me with her roses. It's nice to know that your neighbors think you know what you're doing.

You would be very upset if you knew that Betty was visiting when you are not here. Seeing her just makes your day. Every time you walk out the front door, you go running to the fence we share with Betty and Richard's house. If she's out in the front yard with seven-year-old Bec, you practically have a heart attack jumping and calling out "Betteee, Betteee." You don't get that excited to see me. You just expect me to do everything for you and be there in case you should need anything. It's just like the Queen Bee always said when we were growing up. "All I do is cook and clean. No one cares. No one notices. No thanks. They just take, take, take." Okay, she may have been a bit angry during those early years. Actually, I think she is still angry. It's too bad you have to become a parent yourself to have the curtains open up in your fat, overly critical mind to preview a little movie called "How my parents survived raising four children and why they did the things they did. Part One." It's so easy to judge your parents harshly before you yourself have kids. After all my years of whining, analyzing, critiquing and arrogantly advising my own parents on how they should fix their messy lives, now that I'm on the other side of the fence, I don't think they did such a bad job after all. In fact, the more I experience the "challenges" of parenthood, the more heroic they look for even sticking around.

Today I attended my first Master Gardener class at the Marin Arts and Garden Center. Before I left the house, Papa asked me where my apple was. "What are you talking about?" I said.

"You know, the one you're going to give your teacher."

I drove the back roads, enjoying the beautiful countryside despite the cold, rainy day. Of course, I was the first one to arrive at class. (I didn't tell Papa that because he would've gotten too much enjoyment out of it.) The next goody-goody to arrive was a woman named Rachel. She came over and introduced herself, probably because I looked so pathetic sitting there in the front row, alone. She's from Missouri but had lived in New York City working as an actor for ten years. We reminisced about the gloomy unemployment office in Queens that had not one chair. If you wanted to ever see your money, you had to stand in line for two hours rubbing shoulders with chain smokers, out-of-work truck drivers and very vocal construction workers cursing out the misfortunate clerk who worked the desk. We bonded immediately.

Then the thirty-five other excited gardening geeks arrived. Everyone looked a bit nervous. It felt like the first day of school. We had to put on name tags and stand up and introduce ourselves. Then Tony and Sunshine, our training coordinators, explained the class schedule and the year's program to us eager little beavers. After two hours of taking in information, I was beginning to fade when Sunshine told us that each week we would have a snack period. That woke me right up. I was the first one in the kitchen for coffee and cookies.

After break David Fazzio from Sonoma Nursery lectured us on plant identification. Everyone in the class had been asked to bring in a cutting of a plant we wanted identified. David walked around the room and named the genus and species of each one. He was quite impressive. I began to feel like I knew absolutely nothing about plants. I felt like a fraud even being there. But then I heard a bunch of classmates behind me sighing, looking exasperated and whispering how overwhelmed they felt. I immediately felt better about myself, while questioning whether the others were just a bunch of losers.

And then there's Don.

Don sat behind me and Rachel. He knew almost all the answers. Each time Don disagreed with our lecturer about a certain species, Rachel slowly turned her head to me and stared without saying a word. We're not sure about Don. He knows too much and we are so very jealous.

I'm trying not to be judgmental . . . but I'm sensing some judgment about Don.

I arrived home late and exhausted from a full day of lectures.

On the kitchen table was a brand new loose-leaf binder with a zipper. It has special pockets for pens and highlighters and laminated folders. There was a card on it from Papa saying, "Good luck Goody-Goody," with a red apple sitting on top.

I got up at 4:00 A.M. to film a sunrise shot and worked a long, absurd day in the financial district. We were filming a margarine commercial with Japanese clients who didn't speak any English. The day was filled with guessing games and mind reading among an oddball American director, the stoic Japanese client and an ambiguous translator trying to describe the action in an upcoming shot. At some key moments I thought I was watching a *Saturday Night Live* skit. I arrived home way past your bedtime. After showering, I cuddled with Papa on the couch for a few minutes, while he sat mesmerized by the sports news update. I crept into your room and quietly lifted you out of your crib and tucked you into bed with me. I wrapped you in your blanket, placed you gently on my stomach, and lay back to watch the full moon illuminate the garden. You slept quietly as I held you tight, wondering what I did to deserve you in my life, in my arms.

I almost, for a moment, believed in God.

Our teacher today was Paul Vossen. The class was on the basics of horticulture. We learned about photosynthesis, respiration, translocation and transpiration. These are the processes by which plants get their nutrients, sunlight and water through chemical reactions. We humans forget the symbiotic relationship that humans and plants have. The plants excrete oxygen, which we breathe in, and we exhale carbon dioxide, which they absorb in through their leaves. We need lots of green plants around us to survive. Perhaps a rose obsession isn't such a bad thing after all.

PS Today's snack was brownies. I intended to bring one home for you but I ate it while stuck in traffic. Sorry. By the way, your papa thinks I'm obsessed. He hasn't *seen* obsessed! He should come eavesdrop on some of the chatter that goes on in class. My classmates are gardening addicts! Today I felt as if I were in an obsessed gardeners' support group, and I was one of the relatively sane ones.

That is very, very scary.

Early this morning your papa and I packed you up and delivered you and your belongings (Bunny, blanket and Arthur suitcase) to Grandma Gin-Gin's house so we could go skiing. Thanks for giving "your people" a day off, though it wasn't really your idea. Papa just bought me brand new skis, reminiscent of the time he gave me the gift of rock climbing shoes and a new bike. I wasn't exactly thrilled then either, but as time goes on, I realize he gives me these things so we can enjoy little adventures together. "Enjoying" may not be the right word, actually, as I'm usually about fifty feet behind him, screaming, "I hate your !@#$! guts. I'm going home and I'm never doing this again! I hate the outdoors and all the trees still look alike. . . . Can you hear me? Do you even care? Babe . . . are you ignoring me?"

Complete silence.

Cross-country skiing turned out to be a lot of fun. It was a crisp, sunny day, and my new skis moved swiftly. Pushing and gliding, I kept up fairly well with Mr. Triathlete. My thoughts were of you, of course. Do mothers ever really get away from their children? I think not. I missed you. I was picturing you as you were yesterday. We were in Betty's backyard. I had just finished pruning her roses, when you took off into the street, in your muddy rubber boots, pulling the old, rusty red wagon and chasing Fatcat. In your squeaky little voice you were excitedly clicking your tongue against the roof of your mouth trying to call him, "Ticka-ticka-ticka-ticka-ticka." The closer I got to you, the louder you chimed and the faster you ran, until you ran into a tree.

We skied for a couple of hours and then went to a café to have hot tea. Papa pulled out a map of the Sierras, showing me all the places he wanted to take me skiing. I'm not dying to ski again in the near future, but it was so wonderful to see him happy that I just nodded my head in agreement. That's what really counts. That and how happy I was, because as he was talking about moonlit skiing in the High Sierra, I had cleverly calculated how many calories I had just burned.

Today in class we learned about plant propagation and pruning. A wonderful and knowledgeable instructor named Walter Earle taught us how to sow seeds and make cuttings correctly. The same few classmates who usually get on my nerves, however, kept interrupting him by asking long, elaborate, detailed and ambiguous questions when it wasn't even question time. When Walter gave them an answer they didn't like, they'd keep on talking as if we cared about their opinion! Rachel sighed, turned to me and wrote on my note page, "I think some of our class-mates are postal employees."

Walter owns a nursery in Tomales called Mostly Natives. If it's sunny tomorrow, and if you're in a pleasant mood, maybe you and I will go for a drive in the country and visit. Am I just kidding myself? It's been raining for weeks, you're moody, I have PMS and your favorite word is "no." So we may as well forget that idea. Okay, moving on.

After class Walter brought out four flats of seedlings filled with foxglove, Mexican daisy and fuchsia. He gave us small pots so we could take plants home. Well, you should've seen all thirty-seven geeky Master Gardener trainees trying to contain their excitement. Free plants! That's like giving junkies free heroin!

I pushed and trampled a few of the geriatric classmates to get to the plant table first. (I'm not proud of this quality.) But wouldn't ya know it, fellow trainee Melanie beat me there. Nothing stops Melanie! She's retired but she sure is fast. She sits next to Rachel and me in the front row. We weren't too sure about her at first. She seemed to be having a few too many senior moments. Each week she got all the calendar dates wrong and postponed our snack break by having Tony go over the entire class schedule again. Plus, she hangs with Don, so she may be a Miss Know-It-All too. Not that that's a bad thing. And not that I'm being judgmental.

Today Melanie shared her pretzels and neon highlighters with Rachel and me, so now we like her.

Our pear, apple and plum trees are old and should need little or no pruning by now. However, I've decided I'm going to thin them a bit to open them up to more sunshine and to get more lateral shoots, which is what you want for fruit trees. I also need the practice. You watched me from your swing on the deck as I climbed the ladder and stared at the apple tree, trying to find some inner confidence to begin cutting. The perplexed expression you wore looked just like Papa. This sight would make him cringe too. He can't bear to watch me prune (based on past results), and I can't say I blame him. Initially I follow the diagrams in the pruning book, but then I'm off doing my own thing, pruning without conscience and predictably leaving the sacrificial plant looking butchered and unidentifiably misshapen. For this ex-New Yorker, having a green thumb doesn't necessarily come easy.

Daydreaming thoughts not to have while pruning trees:

1. Childhood Thanksgiving dinners.
2. Irritating phone calls with your mother.
3. Boyfriends who said "I'll call you" twenty years ago and didn't, and you're still pissed.
4. Why your husband is being so quiet.
5. More irritating phone calls with your mother.
6. Why your baby won't sleep through the night.
7. *Exasperating* phone calls with your mother.

Last night, our close friend Cecily slept over with her cute little dog named Patsy. You get very excited when they come to stay with us. You pulled out all of your favorite pillows and blankets and made a big bed on the floor for the three of you. You ran around the backyard annoying poor Patsy to no end, while Cecily and I discussed the film project she recently turned down in Los Angeles. She was distraught and angry. She had brought the script with her. We leafed through the pages together and I kept saying to her, "No, this can't be real. There's a mistake here. What kind of deranged and delinquent producers would hand over forty million dollars to produce a purposeless, graphically violent film that begins with a pregnant bride being beaten by four men in a wedding chapel? This is "art"?

Cecily, who is unemployed and broke, turned down thousands of dollars by not accepting the project. When she phoned her producer friends in L.A. to say she was turning down this Academy-Award-winning director's project because of the violent content, they unanimously told her that it was the biggest mistake of her life, that she was ruining her career and that she was . . . *crazy*. I made her some peach tea and told her how proud I was of her for having the guts to stand alone and the integrity to turn down the reckless producers.

When I went to bed that night, I passed by your room and you and Cecily were sleeping face-to-face with Patsy curled up under the covers, between the two of you. You had your arm out across Cecily's shoulder as if you were comforting her. When she sees your sunny face in the morning light, she will know that she made the right decision and that she is not the crazy one.

I pruned the fig, cherry, pear-apple and plum trees just a bit and they look fine and symmetrical. I think the secret is not to prune too much. Get in, get out and just end it. I almost fainted when Papa actually complimented me on my work. Today he had only genuine, positive feedback, instead of his usual "Can I just make a suggestion?" or, "The only thing I would've done differently . . ."

There must be a game on this afternoon.

Later on, your papa was pruning the jasmine and honeysuckle

outside our bedroom window when he came upon two wasp nests. He showed them to me and explained how the wasps collect the dirt to make a nest. Each nest looks like someone glued a clay plate to the stucco wall and drilled a few holes in it. I have trouble believing that it is possible for a bee to do all this on its own. Of course, growing up in New York City, I once had difficulty comprehending how carrots actually grew in dirt and didn't just show up at the supermarket. It just doesn't register with me that those chubby buzzing wasps have well-defined goals and know what they are doing. It bothers me a bit that all this busy building has been going on right outside my bedroom window. I'm not sure if we should just leave the busy bees alone or call somebody.

This would never happen in New York.

Helpful information from Master Gardener class notes:

Basic seed medium

50 percent vermiculite, 25 percent peat moss, 25 percent perlite. Mix, add seeds and mist.

Pruning perennials

Most flowering shrubs that bloom in the spring form blossoms on wood from the previous year, so after they bloom, prune them back so they can start producing next year's growth. Most flowering shrubs that bloom in the summer form blossoms on new wood from the same year, so these you prune when they are dormant in winter (like roses).

Soil

Seventeen nutrient elements for plant growth
Carbon, hydrogen, oxygen, nitrogen, phosphorous, potassium, calcium, magnesium, sulfur, iron, boron, zinc, manganese, chlorine, copper, molybdenum and nickel.

On a pH scale, 1 is the most acidic soil, 7 is neutral, and 14 is the most alkaline soil. Most plants do best at slightly acidic levels (pH of 6 to 7), where the nutrients are in chemical forms that the plant roots can absorb. When the pH of a soil is too low, it can be adjusted with the addition of lime. When the pH of a soil is too high, it can be adjusted with the addition of sulfur.

Soil saprophytes (bacteria and fungi) are beneficial microorganisms known as decomposers and recyclers that help turn soil into humus as they release plant nutrient elements into simple mineral form. Plant roots cannot absorb nutrients in complex organic forms. The nitrifiers, another group of bacteria, feed on the decaying bodies of the decomposers and convert the organic nitrogen in their dead body tissues into an inorganic form that your garden plants can use. One teeny-tiny gram of soil may contain four billion bacteria, one million fungi, twenty million actinmycetes and three hundred thousand algae.

(Like I believe that. . . .)

Forget-me-not

Botanical name: *Myosotis*
Family: Boraginaceae
"Whaaa-whaa" rating: 1

Tiny, clear blue flowers that easily form a sweet groundcover
that works well behind our showy spring bulbs of daffodils,
tulips, anemones and ranunculus. Grows in damp places
and likes partial shade. Flowers and seeds profusely beginning
in late winter and throughout spring. Has reseeded and
persisted in our yard for years.

FEBRUARY

Soil

Dear Jack,

You and I had a picnic in Golden Gate Park with our friends Gwyneth and Daisy. We watched you and Daisy on the carousel. I videotaped the two of you, going up and down on rainbow-colored antique horses. Then we took the trolley back to the beach. You and Daisy sat together far from us, thrilled to be on a train, pointing out the windows, laughing and ripping off your shoes and unloading sand from your socks.

We pretended we didn't know you. (That was Gwyneth's idea.)

She is busy filming in Los Angeles so much lately that our time together is precious. When we are lucky enough to spend an afternoon together, we can't waste a moment. We cover as many topics as we can without missing a beat. It really is an art and a highly sophisticated communication technique that we have developed in our hectic, overly scheduled lives. Okay, maybe it's not that sophisticated.

In some not-so-sophisticated societies it may even be considered . . . cheap gossip.

In a quiet moment I told Gwyneth I was practicing nonjudgment. She laughed and laughed and laughed. I don't know what is so funny about that. She is obviously very jealous. She thinks I am too much of a New York snob to practice nonjudgment. Especially because I have taught you that, historically, New York City has and will always be "the Center of the Universe." She finds it amusing that I won't tell you the name of the town you live in because I don't want you to know that you are growing up in California and not in Manhattan (i.e., the Center of the Universe).

Now she's going to feel the need to compete with me and prove to me how *nonjudgmental* she is and how it comes to her naturally. Like she is better than me! As if internally she is all Zen because she grew up in the enchanting city of Seattle, spending summers with her family on the glorious San Juan Islands and gazing at the spectacular Olympic Mountains. And I, deep inside, am just another miserable and jaded New Yorker who is still impatiently waiting for the subway at Times Square on a humid sweaty August afternoon at rush hour, trying not to make eye contact with any other irritated, pissed off, foaming-at-the-mouth New Yorker, right on the verge of having a full-blown migraine if the train doesn't come this very minute, and a second away from cursing someone out on the oven-baked platform if they dare rub against me as they make their way through the subterranean crowd, going nowhere but in a hurry.

I don't think I'm so judgmental. I might be opinionated about women's issues, tobacco companies, the NRA and the all-time evil, video game manufacturers. (Oh, here's a great idea! Let's manufacture arcade games for kids that are based on the training games designed for the U.S. Army, with realistic looking guns in the children's hands and people exploding on the screen, and then put them in every mall and movie theater in America so young boys can be even more aggressive little bullets of testosterone and learn how to shoot 'em up! And we'll make millions! Woohoo!)

I may have slipped a bit last night when I was watching the

hypercritical pundit-punks on TV bad-mouthing two female sena-
tors. During the commercials I turned to PBS, where Dr. Wayne
Dyer was lecturing on meditation. I sat there agreeing, breathing
slowly and listening to every gentle word coming out of his mouth.
When I was calm, I would channel-surf back to the pundits on
CNN and instantly forget every peaceful, boring, esoteric slice of
baloney I'd just heard and scream very, very bad words at the TV.

Papa says I have a long way to go.

Our instructor this week was Dennis Poggio from the Marin
Municipal Water District. His lecture and handouts were very
extensive and complicated, and after a while, Rachel and I hit over-
load and couldn't take in another drop of information. So we
began writing little notes to each other, just like in sixth grade.
We'd scribble on a torn-off piece of notebook paper and pass it
under the table to each other. When that got old, I started making
marks on her water notes with my bright-pink highlighter. That got
her mad and she started ignoring me and pretending she was
paying attention.

Then it was finally snack break. The other Ann in class had
made the most delicious chocolate chip cookies. Two of the
women in our class thought that I made them, so they ran up and
complimented me on my exquisite baking skills. (I don't bake.
And if I do bake, I try to avoid all the sugar and fat by mixing in so
many healthy ingredients that the end result looks and tastes more
like something you would display in your rock garden, not put in
your mouth.) Just as the words to clear up the confusion were
coming out of my mouth, the class bell rang and we all scurried
back to our seats. So I had no choice, really. I took full credit for

making the perfect cookies and walked proudly back to my chair! Rachel was sitting there watching me strut, shaking her head.

You began your day early this morning by screaming really loudly *"Betteee"* from your crib. I told you Betty is not home and you had a big fit. So, still in our pajamas, I wrapped you in a blanket and walked over to Betty's house, where I picked you up so that you could peek in her front window. You could see the house was dark and no one was home, and then you were nice to me again. You said, "Ta-too" and I said, "You're welcome . . . knucklehead."

As the day progressed, you just couldn't let go of the "Betty" idea, so we went over in the late afternoon when I sensed another minitantrum about to erupt. Betty was mad at Richard for something and I was mad at your papa for watching too much hockey and then going on-line to read about it on the Internet, and then phoning Mr. Louie to discuss what should have happened in the dumb game instead of paying some attention to *me!* I began complaining to Betty, in a nonjudgmental way of course, how dense men can be at times. Just as I was about to do some venting, we were interrupted by Bec stomping into the kitchen with you proudly following behind her, carrying all her Barbie dolls. She informed us that because she's almost eight years old, she's going to sell all her Barbies at the spring garage sale next month. She'll keep just one Barbie. Because I was a Barbie-crazed girl in my childhood, I found the nonchalant disposal of her Barbies blasphemous and upsetting, but I didn't want her to think I was a weirdo, so I remained calm and aloof.

I said, "And you'll keep one Ken too? Right?"

"No, I pulled Ken's head off."

"Why?" I asked. *God, she's my idol.*

"Because it was loose. I threw it in the garbage."

"Would you like to talk about this?" I asked.

"No, would you like to see Barbie's minivan?"

Today the Queen Bee received a dozen yellow roses for Valentine's Day from your Aunt Augusta. After smelling them over and over, which she thoroughly enjoys doing with roses, she noticed that there were only eleven roses instead of a dozen. She said to me on the phone, "They're all out to get you. You can't trust anyone, especially the florists!" She went on for quite a while how everyone is out to cheat, rob and steal. (Is that just a New York thing?) I suggested that maybe the florist was having a bad day and simply made a mistake. I wanted her to be open to the possibility that maybe someone wasn't out to get her intentionally, and to ask why she can't just be grateful that she got flowers? Well, that set off the firecrackers and all of a sudden it became *my* fault.

Then she hung up on me.

PS You were a pain in the neck today. I'm surrounded by a cranky kid and an exasperating mother. What is it with you people?

I called Aunt Carol. I needed to vent about Ma. She could only talk for a minute. As usual, she was rushing off to work and had to stop at the pharmacy for the Queen Bee's medication, then hit the farthest supermarket possible to purchase the only fruit the Queen Bee found acceptable, and then dash into the busiest beauty store to return the wrong Queen Bee hair color and get the correct brand with more peroxide. Before I could speak, she unloaded this extraneous information on me and then practically in the same breath said she had to rush home from work to have dinner with Scott and then go out dancing with her friends Stacy, Tessa and Beth. And possibly, somewhere in between, do a quick stop at the Queen Bee's apartment to unload groceries, taste her mom's tuna casserole and pose for few quick Valentine's Day photos in front of the heart-shaped casserole. How does she do it, one might ask? I have no idea. She is made of something else—part human, part caretaker, part superhero, part martyr, part lifesaver.

My twin sister Carol is my "life" barometer. I measure just how much "worrying" energy I should put into each day based on how she sounds. She doesn't obsess about the end of the world like I do. She doesn't think of all the possible worst-case scenarios that could happen. She just lives life. I can't even imagine living one single solitary day like that. I would surely self-destruct. I'd be unrecognizable. I'd be mist.

One winter when we were in college, Eric, her adorable Hell's Angel, crank-addicted, pothead, daredevil ex-boyfriend took the two of us and our dog, Fluffy, on what he called "a nice Sunday drive" along an icy, windy, treacherous mountain road in Upstate New York. He then proceeded to get us stuck in a snowdrift on the edge of a steep ravine with the front passenger side of the car hanging off the cliff. He told us not to get out of the car, afraid that the weight change would cause the car to tip over the edge. He carefully extracted himself and ran for help. I sat shivering in the backseat of the car with Fluffy on my lap and watching Carol's face as she sat in the front passenger seat. She didn't even look scared. She looked like it wasn't such a big deal. She smiled and told me not to look at the front of the car that was hanging over the cliff's edge. She said at the count of three we would both slowly open the driver-side doors and jump out, away from the car. She counted, we screamed at the top of our lungs and we jumped.

We were fine and the car didn't even tip over. It was all very uneventful really. We decided that Eric was probably really, really stoned and thought the situation was much worse than it was. In fact, I don't remember him ever coming back to the car. Carol deciphered that Eric, who had a knack for finding a drug deal anywhere, had found junkie-elves back in the forest with some really good homegrown and forgot about us. She got fed up waiting for him and drove the car out of the snowdrift herself.

Now, whenever I am afraid, I call Carol and get her opinion on certain personal situations and world affairs. I call her my "end of the world" gauge. When she says it's the end of the world, we all better run for cover.

❧ ❧

On the way home from the supermarket, we passed a pile of fresh, beautiful wood chips near the deserted railroad tracks. You and I asked a few of the merchants nearby if the wood chips belonged to anyone, but they didn't know. I made a few inquiries by phone when we got home, but the town officials had no idea where the wood chips came from. So there was only one thing to do. Because I wasn't sure if we'd be stealing or doing something else illegal, I called New York Mike.

In his loud New York teamster voice he said, "Who cares who the !@#$! owns it! We found it!" Interesting logic.

Two minutes later he was honking the horn of his pickup truck in front of our house. We brought along your shovel and big rubber boots so you could feel you were part of the project. When we got there, you didn't help much but you sure looked good and that's what counts. Of course, it started drizzling on us sinners, but Mike and I continued filling up his truckbed to the top with wood chips.

You and I spent the afternoon mounding fresh mulch to all the perennials and the roses. Tomorrow another storm is supposed to hit and all of our plants will be tucked in, warm and cozy.

So there we were, your Papa and I at 4:00 A.M. last night, sleeping like babies (the kind that sleep, not you), minding our own business, dreaming of the oriental poppy seeds that had just sprouted, imagining our garden filled with magical red poppies everywhere, when we suddenly woke up to *"whaaaaaaaaa."* It was your favorite the-world-is-coming-to-an-end scream. This middle-of-the-night human alarm clock that shakes the whole house, and quite possibly wakes the dead, has been going on the past few nights since you came down with the stomach flu. Papa takes such good care of you, so patient and so caring. He always has little chitchats with you as he rocks you back to sleep, going down the long list of people who love you. When you had finally had fallen asleep again, Papa came back to bed and we mumbled to each other about how exhausted we were from these past nights of interrupted sleep. I lay there tossing and turning, thinking about the time when you were just a few months old. I had postpartum depression and we were very sleep deprived. One night, after the third or fourth feeding, I stumbled back to bed depleted and snippy. Papa looked at me and said, "You know, I'm tired too. It's time you embraced motherhood."

This was not the best comment to make at that moment. Instead of smothering him with my pillow, I got out of bed in a huff and went to the kitchen to make some warm milk. I sat by the window, which had soft raindrops falling on it, and tried to read a gardening magazine. I was too tired to enjoy it, so I read one of those baby books. I read that chapter on how to get your baby to sleep through the night over and over again. It was difficult to concentrate because I was so utterly exhausted. Everyone had told me I'd lose sleep the first year, but no one told me just how much sleep I'd lose. Everyone told me, "It changes your life," but no one mentioned how much it changes your relationship with your partner.

I had no idea what I had gotten myself into. I stared out the window and wept. I cried because I was sleep-deprived but also because I felt guilty for not being the perfect happy new mother. I didn't talk to many people in those days because I felt that everyone expected me to be thrilled, and I wasn't thrilled. I was sad that I had lost my old life, scared to death of the responsibility of taking care of you, too tired to work in the garden or see my friends and I missed my work (the paying job). I was bored and worn down by the monotony of changing diapers, pumping milk, folding laundry, sterilizing bottles, washing dishes, cleaning the kitchen floor, changing sheets, pumping more milk, doing more laundry, food shopping, trying to cook a decent meal, trying to return a phone call, trying to squeeze in a nap, changing more diapers, folding more laundry and hardest of all, trying to be pleasant and chipper at the end of the day. I was jealous of Papa because he could escape to work. He wasn't expected to just drop his career or change his life as dramatically as I had. And because I had been socially conditioned by outdated religion and other spooky patriarchal institutions that say women's primary purpose is to have children and to serve her husband and her children (*say what?*), I felt guilt-ridden for not being the perfect selfless little caretaker generously ready to give.

I knew exactly what was missing.

I soon realized that I had meant to order the deluxe package. The one that came with a wife. I just needed a wife.

It was that simple.

When I came back to bed, Papa was still awake. He said, "Can you imagine those people who have a baby thinking it's going to *save* their marriage?" And for what seemed like the first time in weeks, we howled with laughter, at other people's expense, of course. Then I told him that I didn't think I was ready to embrace motherhood, especially since he had suggested it. (If I had come up with it on my own, I may have considered it. Well, actually, now that I think about it, that is highly unlikely.)

I think you can love your child more than anything in the world but you can't always love being a mother. The hours are long, the job is emotionally confusing, you get a lot of lip service about doing the most important job in the world yet there's no real tangible recognition and people still wonder what it is you do all day. And worst of all, no matter what your child turns into later in life, *you'll* be blamed.

Today at naptime you fell asleep in my arms in the rocking chair. When I tiptoed into your room to put you into your crib, you opened your eyes for a second, looked up at me and fell back to sleep with a smile on your face. I think you'll feel better soon.

Master Gardening class today was going to be about "pests" but class was cancelled because of the torrential rain and windstorm. I stayed home and looked at the pest pictures in our textbook: wildlife pests like squirrels, voles, moles, rabbits, birds and other rodents. First of all, Jack, if I ever got remotely close to a rodent in our garden, I would probably faint. Second, this reminds me of the pesky little birds that came to the poor old privet tree, so I'm going to tell you that story.

Once upon a time, when I was pregnant with you, we had a privet tree outside our bedroom window. One day a family of squeaky birds decided to move into that tree and hold big parties at 2:00 A.M. with lots of loud tweety-bird guests. This went on for weeks. Your papa and I would go out there in the middle of the night and spray them with the water hose or throw pebbles at them, but they didn't care. They just kept on squeaking, singing up a storm. So, one day when Papa went to work, I did what any reasonable, pregnant, irascible New Yorker, who thinks all trees look alike, would do: I had the privet tree cut down.

And the birds went away.

And all was well.

Today in class we learned about plant pathology with Dr. Robert Raabe, who is so adorable and bright that we all wished he was our long-lost European uncle. He began his lecture by stating, "I have a fantastic disease collection in my own garden." I fell in love with him from that moment on because he made us feel it was okay not to have perfect plants in our gardens. Some level of disease will always be there. It's just part of being a living thing. The really severe or contagious diseases are what you want to contain. I asked him about our lavatera and our tomato plants, which all have Verticillium wilt, the soilborne fungus that attacks plants and their roots, restricting water flow and causing the plants to wilt and eventually die. He suggested planting resistant varieties or soil solarization. This is a process you would use during the hottest time of the summer. You cover your infected soil box with clear plastic, which traps heat and moisture at levels lethal to many weed seeds as well as to many fungi and pest organisms. I'm going to try it this summer. He said if that doesn't work, there is only one other way to get rid of soil-borne fungus: "Move."

I'm telling you, Jack, after three hours of hearing about sixteen hundred species of bacteria, one hundred thousand known species of fungi, a plethora of plant pathogenic viruses and satellite viruses, parasitic nematodes and twenty-five hundred species of parasitic seed plants, I left class feeling sick about our whole diseased garden.

What's the use? Assassins surround us. We're doomed.

The infectious disease triangle:
To develop an infectious disease, there must be three compatible essential components.

    1. A pathogen in contact with the host plant.
    2. A susceptible host plant.
    3. An environment favorable to the pathogen.

Soil solarization
In July remove all weeds from plant boxes. Till or rake the soil free of clumps, prepare the soil for planting and level the soil. Water the soil. Purchase a *clear* tarp. Transparent plastic will allow more heat

to penetrate than colored tarps will. Polyethylene plastic one millimeter thick works best, but two millimeters could be used in windy areas. Roll tarp out over the soil. Smooth out air pockets. Wait four to six weeks in full sun for maximum treatment and remove plastic. Plant new disease-resistant plants.

Magnolia

Botanical name: *Magnolia*
Family name: Magnoliaceae
"Whaaa-whaa" rating: 4

Magnolias were one of the first plants on earth to reproduce using flowers pollinated by insects. Magnolias prefer full sun in rich, moist, well-drained soil. Most are slow growers but will grow into very large trees. These ancient beauties have showy white, pink or burgundy upright magnificent tulip-shaped fragrant flowers.

Need deep and regular watering. Two magnolias that do well in Northern California are the star magnolia (*Magnolia stellata*) and the saucer magnolia (*Magnolia soulangiana*). The one we see in the South is the *Magnolia grandiflora*, which blooms in the summer.

MARCH

Bugs

Dear Jack,

This weekend Papa and I took you bike riding on the rural, rolling hills near the cheese factory. We traded you back and forth so we each had a chance to sing your little songs with you and watch you get excited at seeing the horses, cows and birds. You're beginning to know the words to "You Are My Sunshine," which Grandpa plays on his harmonica for you while you dance. Papa and I had fun speeding on our bikes, trying to complete a whole sentence before being interrupted by your demands for more farm animals. We're getting so good at this that we actually achieved headway in our conversations and made some good plans for future garden projects.

I'm sitting in the sunny garden, next to the first ten bright-pink species tulips that just opened, reading my entomology notes. I usually read my Master Gardener books at night after you go to bed, but this week the reading is all about: *insects!* The pictures in the book bother me so much that I have nightmares, so I have to read these chapters in daylight. When I was reading about fireflies, I thought about you and about how you are in constant motion. Fireflies use their lights (luciferin) to find one another. Female fireflies just sit still in one place flashing their lights while the male fireflies flutter all around in an adolescent frenzy.

As I'm sitting here trying to stay calm, with each graphic microscopic color photo of the insect world, an earwig has just crawled out of my notebook. Of course I jump across the deck screaming and throwing all of my textbooks and notebooks up in the air. Both Maui and Fatcat jump up from their peaceful afternoon naps, wondering what to do next with their mundane useless lives. Could they chase a few earwigs? Is that asking too much?

Today we spent three hours trapped in a classroom, itching, looking at slides of insects. Our instructor was Stacy Carlson. He is our county agricultural commissioner as well as an entomologist. Please do not become one of these. You'll spend your whole life itching, and anyone who finds out what you do for a living will immediately begin itching too.

There are close to one million different species of insects on the planet. Worldwide, only about ten thousand species are considered pests. The majority of insects are either beneficial or "neutral" (e.g., bees pollinate plants, other insects prey on pest insects). The best thing you can do to encourage beneficial insects in your garden is to avoid the use of pesticides whenever possible. This way you do not upset the ecological balance between pests and their natural enemies.

So there I was, sitting in the front row of the class for the entire afternoon, watching these close-up slides of a few beautiful bugs and lots of disgusting, scream-worthy, nightmare-inducing ones. If people knew just how many creepy-crawlers there were living right outside their front door, they'd never leave their homes. In fact, Rachel, who looked more than once like she was ready to faint, and I decided that we might never step out into our gardens again. After two hours of insect slides I started closing my eyes and hiding. I just couldn't take any more. When Mr. Carlson got to the American cockroach, I jumped out of my seat and went outside to get some air.

It was pouring rain but I didn't care. I just wanted to escape the insect world. I stood under the awning, pondering how this topic could be absolutely fascinating and equally repulsive at the same time. I was just about to lean on the brick staircase when I spotted a whole colony of ants speeding up the wall on a mission. I knew it. I should've stayed inside. They're everywhere. When I went back into the classroom, we were on the grand finale of slides, the venomous arthropods. (Spiders have eight eyes!) I could handle those better than the cockroaches. Growing up in New York, center of the universe, we were so busy running from cockroaches, that we'd probably have never noticed a black widow or fuzzy brown recluse, or believed that they only existed in foreign countries, like . . . Iowa.

Just finished a grueling car shoot with a teenybopper, narcissistic director and a sneaky, noncommunicative, vindictive cameraman. So there I was, stuck between two pubescent amateurs for a week, one whining on each side of me. These two skinny geeks are supposedly the latest rave in television commercial production. Where is it written that in order to be a "creative genius" you have to be a difficult, spoiled, ungrateful *freak!?*

Is it really asking too much to be talented and act normal at the same time?

The last day of the job, while the director, Mr. Teenybopper, was filming a dangerous sunset shot from a helicopter above us, I got into a fight with the cameraman, Mr. Sneaky. We were filming a complicated car chase sequence directly below the helicopter on a camera car driving fast on a windy, slippery mountain road on Mount Tamalpais. Walkie-talkie transmission between me and the California Highway Patrol officers began to fail. They couldn't hear me trying to lock up traffic, and the helicopter crew above couldn't hear me trying to contact them. All I heard over my walkie-talkie was a bunch of static interspersed with the director's whiny voice screaming, "Keep shooting. Just keep shooting!"

Realizing that the road was still open to pedestrian traffic, and that an old Mercury Comet with two surfboards on the top and two hippies below was speeding toward us, I quickly shut down the shoot. We drove back to base camp and immediately wrapped for the day. The entire way down the mountain Mr. Sneaky, whose camera crew spent most of their day plotting a mutiny, and I argued with each other. He wanted to keep filming. I knew we had already got the necessary sunset shots from the camera car and the helicopter, and I felt that it was too dark and too unsafe to continue filming more than we really needed. But mostly I was sick and tired of him. We were both strapped onto the camera car, so I couldn't get away from him! I had to hear him whine, whine, whine, just like a spoiled two-year-old throwing a tantrum because he didn't get his way, all the way down the mountain. *Whaa, whaa, whaa!*

When we got down to base camp, he ran right over to Mr. Teenybopper and squealed on me. It was happy hunting ground. The two of them stood there commiserating because the big mean lady took away their toys. What a bunch of babies!

The next day the commercial's producer had an enormous bouquet of flowers delivered to me and to Gwyneth, who was the other assistant director on the shoot. It's just like my producer friend Lope says, "I knew it was going to be a bad shoot. But I didn't think it was going to be absurd and stupid as well."

Early this morning Papa and I dropped you off at Grandma Gin-Gin's house so we could sneak away skiing with Mr. Louie and Pucci. You are teething again, we think. If all else fails, our motto is "Blame it on molars coming in." You've been pretty cranky and exhausting to be around the past few days, so we're doing what any other dysfunctional parent would do—running away. Skipping town! If we didn't get away for some rest and fun in our lives, we were going to have to quit our jobs as "your people." We drove out to Ice House Road in the Sierras with Pucci and Mr. Louie. We spent the car ride there telling stories, laughing, reading the newspaper, eating potato chips and listening to our choice of music, instead of "The Wheels of the Bus Go Round and Round." Not that it's not a nice song, and not that I'm being judgmental.

It was the sunniest day we've had in weeks—clear skies, bright warm sun and perfect snow. We cross-country skied for four hours. Pucci and I solved all of our family issues and half the world's problems while your Papa and Mr. Louie discussed hockey and football the entire time. They were determined to solve the problems of their favorite sports teams—such caring and compassionate men.

We got back to Grandma Gin-Gin's house around 5:00 P.M. We had a great day, but it sure was nice coming home to you. Your Grandma always tells me how easy you are and what a great time she had. I can never, ever complain to her about the hardships of caring for *one* baby because she had eight children. Though she is far too polite and kind, I imagine her rolling on the floor laughing at the notion that I find raising one child *challenging*.

She said you took a three-hour nap. You would never even consider sleeping that long at home. Your subconscious mind would blast an alarm off as loud as a foghorn to alert you that "your people" have stopped moving, are relaxing, having a grown-up conversation (most probably about you), and that you must get up immediately to continue the task of wearing us down.

Have I told you about hardenbergia? Hardenbergia is an Australian vine that has beautiful clusters of purple pea-like flowers. It blooms in late winter to early spring. In our garden it is one of the first flowers to open after the cold, wet and dreary winter. Papa and I get very excited when the hardenbergia begins to bloom. It is a sign that spring is just around the corner. Soon enough we will be out in the garden checking up on everything, celebrating each plant that survived the winter and rating them in the Universal Botanical "whaaa-whaa" rating system.

Last week, after our two prolific hardenbergias on the deck began to bloom so magnificently, Papa became a bit obsessed. He went out to the nursery and bought two more five-gallon plants. He set them in huge clay pots and placed them strategically around our garden so that in every direction you look, there's a big, tall, blooming hardenbergia smiling back at you.

Betty was here yesterday commenting on how nice the backyard looks and telling us how excited she gets each spring waiting to watch our garden begin to bloom. Papa and I were so thrilled and shocked to have someone compliment us on our garden that we decided not to tell her we had just purchased the two new hardenbergias that were making the garden look so alive. We didn't want to disappoint her. It's so nice to have someone think we know what we're doing.

Why ruin it?

❧ ❧

My old friend Annie, a movie propmaster from New Jersey, is out visiting us. We met while working on a movie crew many years ago. She's the reason I know all the words to "Louise" that I sing you to sleep with. One drunken night at 3:00 A.M., after a wrap party in a swank Florida hotel room, Annie sang it to me eleven times and then passed out.

You two immediately bonded. Her favorite color is purple, just like yours. She lets you play with the electric windows in her rented Jeep. You are in heaven. She just came back from spending a week working at the Tassajara Zen Center, getting the place in order for the summer guests. It's a spiritual retreat hidden in the Carmel Mountains, a place that the Queen Bee, if she knew of it, would definitely shake her head at and classify as a "cult." But Annie came back looking so calm and happy. She was one of the people in charge of a work crew that did the painting, cooking, cleaning and gardening. She told me it was hard for her to have incompetent free labor to assign jobs to. In the film business, if you show any sign of weakness in your area, your replacement arrives before you're even told to hit the road! The monks at the Zen Center told Annie that if they find people lacking at their jobs, they keep them for at least five years and then gently and kindly move them to another department.

It is an unseasonably warm day, so we pulled out your little pool in the backyard. I'm trying to keep things calm out here in the backyard so Annie can still feel the tranquility of last week, but you are making it difficult. You are racing around naked, jumping in and out of your pool, screaming, "Jump!" You are splashing her and I am ruining her day by telling her that this warm weather is a sure sign of the apocalypse and the depleting ozone layer and that we should all have listened to Al Gore. She rolls her eyes and tells me in her sarcastic New Jersey non-Zen tone that I haven't changed a bit. I tell her about yesterday's visit to Mostly Natives Nursery in Tomales, where you and I took a road trip on a wonderfully mysterious foggy day. Besides the abundance of native plants, they have old Radio Flyer wagons in which to put the plants you plan to purchase. You went wild over the wagon and, of course, demanded that you be allowed to lug it around, almost destroying entire sections of perennials at every turn. Walter Earle, who was our propagating teacher in the Master Gardener class, is the owner. I stopped and talked with him for a while about some tall grasses that I wanted to get for our yard. I'm trying to be more diverse and not just get plants that have beautiful flowers, but plants that add some contrast or have interesting foliage. The conversation obviously went on too long by your standards and you began pulling all the name tags out of the plants and tossing them into the sky.

I was so embarrassed. I went to grab you and you ran away. There I was chasing you around this tranquil nursery in this calm little town looking exactly like those frantic mothers I made fun of and judged all my life. *I am so sorry for judging!* The two women who worked there were trying to be polite, but I could tell they wanted you gone as soon as humanly possible. Walter just kept deadheading his plants, immersed in his own little world. Every few cuts he'd look up and glance at me chasing you. I couldn't tell whether he thought you were cute or that I was an incompetent mother not in control of my bratty child. After I finally captured you and tossed you over my shoulders, I locked you in your car seat while I went to pay for the plants we bought.

You and I made peace when we found a trampoline across the street in a small park. You jumped for twenty minutes straight, while I read about my new clematis Montana, which has sweet flowers that look like anemones. I watched you jumping and laughing. Do you ever stop moving? I'll pay you to stop, I swear. You would've kept going but I got tired of watching you, so I grabbed you and locked you in your car seat and drove home. You were asleep in about two minutes.

Sweet victory!

You just now ran over to Annie's lounge chair dripping wet, jumping naked all around her, yelling, "Annie, where can I jump? Where can I jump?"

In her loud, tough New Jersey accent she said, "Off a bridge, Jack. Off a bridge."

Papa and I just celebrated our "day we met" anniversary. It was eleven years ago at a party in San Jose. Aunt Carol had just graduated from chiropractic school, and I had flown out from New York to celebrate with her. This is where I met your extended family— Charlie, Tracey, Ron, Barbara and Wendy—for the first time. The party was at Terry Shroeder's house. He is an Olympic water polo silver medalist and fellow chiropractor. Everyone at his house looked really athletic, sun baked and . . . happy? I was a lonely, dark, angry New Yorker dressed in black. I was standing near the Queen Bee, who was sitting on her throne at the front door of Mr. Gold Medalist's suburban home, interrogating people as they came in. She was worse than the Mafia. With each guest who entered the front door, she chirped: "Do you belong here? You don't look right. Don't tell me you're a doctor too? You look like a little-kittle. Who are you kidding? Are you Jewish?"

Aunt Augusta and I were taking turns on duty. We were in charge of bringing our mother Diet Cokes and Bloody Marys and keeping her company so she didn't embarrass Aunt Carol by yelling at her in that "I'm your mother" tone in front of her peers. The Queen Bee kept asking me and anyone else in earshot, "Why are you wearing a black dress on such a sunny day? What a shmate! Don't you have any solid-color pastels? Would it kill you to wear a cheerful color? Bright orange would look good on you." Then she'd stare at me, shaking her head. I was still in my I-hate-everyone-especially-men-and-my-mother phase, during which I only wore black, but she didn't quite get the concept. Finally I left my post exasperated and went to grab a beer from the fridge. There was your Papa leaning on the kitchen counter, discussing the 1917 Armenian massacre with Aunt Augusta in extensive detail. We locked eyes for a moment. I thought he was cute but he looked way too healthy for my taste—and way too interested in one of Aunt Augusta's lengthy, philosophical explanations of world history that left the listener dizzy and speechless, wondering why she just answered a question with another question?

I'd hate to ruin my track record of dating only moody, drug-addicted, alcoholic, emotionally unavailable men, I thought to myself.

When Augusta finally wrapped up her loquacious dissertation on world peace, he was clearly in need of some depthless conversation so he headed over my way and we began talking about a movie he had seen with my name in the credits. Aunt Carol had told him about her workaholic twin sister who had sold her soul to the atrocious movie industry and lived a lonely, angry existence, dateless, in Manhattan. (Thanks, Carol.) He asked many questions about my career, and we talked about my favorite subject—me— for twenty minutes. We talked briefly about his chiropractic career and his interest in getting his acupuncture license and then it was back to, you guessed it, me! I was trying not to look ecstatic that I was actually having a normal conversation with a normal guy till reality hit.

My mother called out at an earsplitting level above the party noise, "Annie, I'll have another Bloody Mary! Without all that salt. Your snippy sister won't bring me another. Why is my diabetes her business? She's like the police. Uch, who is that cute Goy-toy you're talking to so long? What's wrong with him?"

When Papa came home from work tonight, you began crying and demanded that he pick you up and not put you down. I tried to make a nice dinner but accidentally spilled half the pepper shaker into the soup while trying to clean your hands of the chocolate pudding you were about to smear all over the kitchen wall. We stupidly tried to have a quiet anniversary dinner with you along. What were we thinking?

The soup was too spicy to even be near, let alone eat. The salmon was cold and the salad had gotten soggy because we had to wait to eat because you needed the "correct" spoon, fork and bib, which were all dirty. I calmly washed them and set them on the table. You then threw your whole clean setting on the floor. You got a big fat time-out in your room while Papa and I inhaled our food in five minutes, knowing this was going to be our only peaceful time to eat, even though you were wailing in the background. We were both so drained that we had not one thing to say to each other. We ate our horrible anniversary dinner, silently did the dishes and went to bed.

I couldn't sleep because I was too upset, so I called Aunt Sha. She had just bought an expensive white little fluffy dog, named Spot, for Cousin Rebecca. She's had him a few days and now she is realizing that Spot is *deaf*. This is very ironic because Sha is so *loud!* She speaks in capital letters only. At work they beg her to use her indoor voice. I got back into bed laughing at the thought of Sha having a deaf dog. I find that so satisfying. And while I'm on the topic of my big sister Sha, who I couldn't possibly live without, let me add one more thing. When we were kids, she wouldn't let Carol and I play with her Barbie dolls. When we went to our big cousin Sue's house for sleepovers, Sue and Sha got to play with all the good stuff in Barbie's dream house while Carol and I were locked in the attic with old torn paper dolls from the last century with ninety-five-year-old Nanny walking around with her proverbial jar of mustard threatening to paint our fingers if we bit our nails or sucked our thumbs. I still have nightmares about it. And I still wonder how it is possible that wherever and whenever we played Monopoly with Sha, she always had to be banker and she *always* won.

Purely coincidental? I think not.

A few weeks ago, when I was visiting her in L.A., we hired a babysitter for you and Cousin Rebecca so we could escape midday and catch a matinee. We sat in our seats, beaming, like two kids who were playing hooky from school. The show was at a newly built, state-of-the-art Hollywood Cineplex. When we finished giggling and doing high-fives about how free it felt to be off-duty moms, we looked up and realized that the screen was the size of a football field. Sha started yelling, "The screen's *too big*. What's *wrong* with these people? Why would they build such a *big screen!!*"

I fell asleep missing her.

On the set today, when I was rushing the director, Randy, a bit too much and suggesting that he stop milking the shot with twenty more perfect takes, he turned to me and said, "You know what, Spiegelman? You're the only woman I know that motherhood has made *less* patient."

❧ ❧

The authors of our botany textbook were trying desperately to say something positive about weeds, and you could tell they were having trouble coming up with anything. Here are the seven redeeming features they mention, in between twenty pages on how to search and *destroy* your weeds:

1. Reduction of dust and erosion.
2. Cover and food for vertebrates, such as birds.
3. Nectar source for honeybees.
4. Habitat for beneficial predators/parasites.
5. Source of additional soil/organic matter.
6. Potential source of therapeutic pharmaceuticals.
7. Source of employment for people hired to control/ remove them.

Weeds are considered "weeds" when they interfere with the intended use of land and water resources. The simplest definition is "a plant growing where it is not wanted." Weeds compete with crops for space, nutrients, water and light.

The philosophy of the Master Gardeners is to control weeds in a way that is least harmful to humans and the environment and to use chemical control only as a last resort. This is all fine and dandy but very difficult to achieve, especially because weed seeds can remain viable in the soil for many years. The example given in our book shows just one mullein plant that had 223,200 seeds! After thirty-eight years, 48 percent of the seeds were still viable. We have to work so hard to prevent viruses, fungi and big ugly parasitic bug infestations, and now 223,200 mullein seeds?

What's the use?

Papa looked over my notes. He told me that he thinks even if we diligently weeded by hand, put down black fabric and paved it over with concrete, we'd still have Bermuda grass in the rose garden.

I call him my doomsday soothsayer. When I start my psychic gardening call-in show on cable TV, he certainly won't be a guest.

We just had a surprise visit today from Chatty Cathy. Have I told you about Chatty Cathy? She's a woman who owns some kind of garden business on the Internet. She lives nearby and knows I'm a gardener. You and I were napping peacefully in the early afternoon. I got out of bed to spend some quiet time with Papa in the kitchen. All of a sudden I saw Chatty Cathy walking down the driveway, so I ran into the office and hid under the desk. Papa answered the door and said I was resting. She handed him some gardening brochures and some good information on native plants. She asked if she could take a look around the garden to see the tulips and some other flowers that are beginning to show an iota of potential. She must have wandered around for twenty minutes passing by each window of each room of our tiny house. I could hear her walking on the deck, right outside the window by the desk I was huddled under like a little mouse. Papa came by every few minutes and simply shook his head.

He thinks I avoid people.

The yard is beginning to show some promise. Many of the roses have buds on them and the orange and pink tulips look magical. The pink jasmine outside our bedroom window is just about to bloom. Forget-me-nots have reseeded all over the backyard. The cinerarias out front are just about to open and the jessamine vine climbing along the trellis on the deck is blooming with so many yellow blossoms it makes the backyard feel radiant and full of light even on a cloudy day. Each year Papa and I get just as excited as the year before watching the garden begin its spectacular springtime bloom. We run around here like two kids, pointing out our favorite blossoms and taking full credit for whatever plant looks the best, whether we had anything to do with its development or not.

It's 2:00 P.M. You know how I know that? Because the house wren just sang on the new bird clock your papa bought for you. As you will come to see over the years, this gift is very typical of your papa. It goes along with the wilderness flannel sheets he just gave you and the moose comforter he gave me. Of course you love the bird clock and each time another bird sings on the hour, you run into the room joyously chiming, "Bird clock!"

Since we've had this bird clock, I've been forced to learn the somewhat melodious yet mostly irritating songs of twelve native birds. I now realize that mockingbirds were the annoying birds that kept me awake last summer and motivated me to cut down the poor old privet tree. Every day at 2:00 P.M., the mockingbirds haunt me by singing their cranky little song on the bird clock. Thousands of little privet tree volunteers have sprouted all around the garden to remind me that I may have won the battle but by no means have I won the war.

Yesterday at sunset you helped me place fifteen hundred lady beetles in the rose garden. When I went out there this morning, hoping to find fewer aphids, I found instead several billion aphids, four dead ladybugs, two live ones and one big couch-potato slug, who looked like he had just finished Thanksgiving dinner and couldn't budge an inch, on my favorite rosebush, Bibi Maizoon.

All in all, Jack, I think our little science experiment was a bust.

Notes from Master Gardener class

Best way to identify an insect on your plant:

Determine if the pest insect has antennae and/or wings. Insect pests have chewing or sucking mouth parts. Distinguish which mouth part it has. Chewing insects (borers, leafminers) eat their way through a plant, leaving holes in leaves, twigs, fruit and stems. Sucking insects (aphids, scales, thrips, whiteflies) use their stylet to suck out plant sap. Symptoms may be curling, stunting or deformed plant parts due to the deprivation of photosynthesis.

Predatory mites, parasitic nematodes, trichogramma wasps, green lacewings and lady beetles are all beneficials that can be purchased and released in the home garden.

Seventy-five percent of all living things on earth are insects.

Beneficial insects you can buy:

Lady beetles: Eat aphids. Release in springtime at dusk. Most of them will fly away to your neighbor's house, but it could be a fun experiment. Insecticidal soap is better for long-term care.

For aphids, a strong force of water from a garden hose a few times is often adequate. (Aphids are attracted to stressed plants.)

Lacewings: Natural enemies of aphids, spider mites, leaf- or bud-eating caterpillars.

Praying mantis: Good predators but not specific eaters, so could eat beneficial insects too. Interesting to watch.

Parasitic wasps: A variety of tiny wasps can be purchased for control of aphids, scales, white fly, caterpillars and some pest eggs.

Ants: Help pollinate plants, recycle nutrients and aerate soil. They are a good source of food because they stay abundant when prey is scarce. They store insects and seeds, use honeydew for energy and even cannibalize their own brood when short of food. They attack termites. When you see ants protecting aphids, put a sticky barrier around the tree trunk. Then use insecticidal soap on the aphids.

Snail and slug control: Copper barriers work well around raised beds.

Earwig control: Persistently placing tuna fish cans filled with vegetable oil will over time reduce populations. One good thing about earwigs is, after they eat all your leaves, they also feed on pest insect eggs and aphids.

Least toxic and safest pesticides:

Pyrethrum, bacillus thuringiensis (Bt), horticultural oils and insecticidal soap.

Sweet Scented Geranium

Botanical name: *Pelargonium graveolens*
Family: Geraniaceae
"Whaaa-whaa" rating: 2

What we puttering gardeners call "geraniums," pedantic
horticulturists refer to as "pelargoniums." Originally discovered
in South Africa, pelargoniums were sent by the botanist Francis
Masson by the hundreds back to Europe in 1772. The legend
goes that he was chased through the African bush by a chain
gang of escaped convicts, almost killed in a hurricane off Saint
Lucia and captured by French pirates on his way back to North
America. For all his bravery and scientific exploration, Masson
received one hundred pounds annually and had a rare lily,
the Massonia, named after him. Poor guy.
Rose-scented geranium *(Pelargonium capitatum)* is one of
my favorite shrubby perennials. The fuzzy leaves have an
intoxicating scent throughout the year. Small light pink
flowers bloom in summer. Grows to three feet tall and
does best in full sun to partial shade. This plant is a must
for rose addicts.

the air so enchanting that I got hoodwinked into believing any-thing was possible.

I've been so impatient with you the past few days. I'm working on my Master Gardener final exam. The minute we put you to bed at night, I go into the kitchen and study for two hours. Last night I was so involved and focused that I burned the popcorn and the pot on the stove, almost starting a fire. Papa didn't care about the house burning down, all he cared about was disconnecting the smoke alarm fast enough so it didn't wake you up.

Thank God he's got his priorities straight.

PS Spoke to Aunt Sha this evening. I told her I was going organic in the garden. There was silence on the phone. She probably was wondering why anyone would get so excited about their garden, and what the heck does *organic* mean anyway? She asked me to look for a plastic leaf cleaner next time I'm at Home Depot, to clean her dust-prone *plastic* plants.

You just got out of a nice warm bath and are now running around the house howling and squealing. Today I am madly in love with you. Yesterday, however, I was not. We had been visiting our extended family at Charlie and Tracey's house in Santa Cruz. You decided you were not going to take a nap or sleep through the night. "Your people" and everyone else staying at our motel were up most of the night listening to you cry.

The next morning I was irascible and a bit out of sorts. Your papa was supposed to have some time alone with his best friends, Ron and Charlie, but half an hour into their time together, I unexpectedly screeched the car into Charlie's driveway. I literally tossed you into Papa's arms and practically threw your car seat at Ron, who was standing on the sidewalk looking very, very scared and useless. I drove off without an explanation. I went into downtown Santa Cruz and wandered around an old bookstore. I sat on a small wooden bench in the photography aisle, looking through beautiful black and white photography books. I came upon a picture of a mother and baby boy. It made me miss you so. I felt so depleted, codependent and confused.

When I arrived back at Charlie's house, Charlie, Ron and Naomi were relaxing in the garden. When I asked where you were, they said Papa was driving you around the block trying to get you to take a nap. He does a lot of that lately—a lot of late-night drives, just you and your driver. While we waited for you to return, Charlie cheered me up by packing up cuttings of his supernatural plants. It is truly amazing that whenever we visit Charlie and he gives us plant cuttings, they always survive the three-hour ride home, some shoved on the dark car floor mat with their roots barely touching water or soil. Then they flourish for years in our garden.

You finally slept, missing the stunning coastal ride home up Highway 1 at sunset. Papa and I talked and listened to a local beach station that played only surf music and gave very serious minute-by-minute updates on surf conditions. We found it hysterically funny. During the entire drive home we switched back and forth between two topics. One was the book Papa was reading about the compassionate teachings of the Dalai Lama. The other was maliciously plotting how many five-gallon blooming perennials we needed and how much money we were willing to spend to make our garden look absolutely breathtaking before Charlie's visit to our house next month.

My mother just hung up on me again. She beat me to the draw. I was just about to slam dunk the phone! I hate when she gets in the last word. I quickly packed up a lunch and my books for class and instead of getting myself into a panic over her like I usually do, I focused on the field trip our class was going on to Green Gulch Farm. I thought about your grandpa and the times I've taken him to the Green Gulch garden. Sometimes we'll just sit on a bench in the garden and watch the Buddhist monks drift through on their way to the Zendo. Other times we'll take walks on the trail to Muir beach, discussing what dessert we would eat if it was our last day on earth or how to cook the perfect lamb chop or make the perfect egg salad sandwich. Sometimes we'll talk about spirituality. I tell him the little I know about Buddhism. He says he likes a religion that gives you plenty of opportunity to nap. Many times he's fallen asleep in the sun, sitting on a bench overlooking the fields of the vegetable garden. When he suddenly wakes up, he tries to convince me he was "meditating." I don't tell him he was sleeping tightly and snoring really loudly.

When I was nine months pregnant with you and I stopped working, I used to come to this garden to sit quietly, breathe, steal ideas for our yard and think about the reality of actually being a mother. I couldn't imagine it and I was petrified. Jack, you can't even fathom the denial I was in. People would give me teeny tiny, absolutely adorable baby clothes for you as gifts, and I would put them in a drawer, thinking, "Oh, now aren't these cute? *Somebody's* having a baby!" Then I'd go about my busy day as if things were just ordinary and *somebody* else was about to have a baby any day. Good for them!

Wendy Johnson was our teacher at Green Gulch. She is in charge of the flower gardens and was a dedicated student of the legendary horticulturist Alan Chadwick. She immediately stated, "We don't proselytize here about Zen, but we do proselytize about compost." She had our entire class of thirty-five students help build the farm's enormous compost pile. They achieve this by adding layers of green to brown (nitrogen to carbon). All the piles of organic trash are organized and methodically planned out. It looks so impressive that for a moment you forget they are piles of garbage. As I was digging and piling on layers of compost, I thought about you. I thought about how you've changed my life. I thought about your papa and how I missed our relationship before you. It has changed so much and has become harder. I realized that I keep trying to hold on to how it used to be but, sooner or later, you have to accept change and stop fighting it.

Today, five feet up, on top of the greatest, smelliest compost pile I've ever stood on, I think I got the message. It hit me while I was overlooking fields and fields of newly planted greens, with the sun breaking through the clouds after the morning shower. I was having this huge revelation about life being ephemeral and kaleidoscopic, when all of a sudden, Mr. Know-It-All, Don, missed the carbon pile and his shovel full of stinky, wormy, bug-infested brown crap came flying in my face.

The Queen Bee calls you and Cousin Rebecca "Buba." I think it means "doll" in Russian. It's her term of endearment for her grandchildren. So, now on your own, you've started calling her

"Grandma Buba." That makes her happy. This morning I said to you, "Let's call the Queen Bee," just checking to see what goes on in that brain of yours. I asked you, "Do you know who the Queen Bee is?" You matter-of-factly said, "Grandma Buba." I'm not sure if it's normal for a young child to know that his Grandma is referred to as the Queen Bee but one day, when you grow up, you can discuss it in therapy.

Today was our last Master Gardener's class. We spent most of the class going over our two-hundred-question final exam. It was good to go through and learn the right answers. But it soon became slow torture, as all the know-it-alls tediously argued with the scientifically-based answers of Tony, our training coordinator. Every ten minutes somebody had a problem with the correct answer. The only thing that kept me from getting up, strangling all the big mouths and leaving was the homemade chocolate chip cookies "the nice" Ann had brought in for snack time. I couldn't wait for snack time! I had studied, done well on the exam and felt that I deserved a treat. The only thing that was standing between me and the cookies were the smart alecks who had to be right about everything. After three hours of this, Rachel turned to me and said, "Somebody has to kill them, plain and simple. That's the only way we'll get our chocolate chip cookies."

Her priorities are so right on!

You are now sitting on the deck eating one of those delicious cookies I brought home this afternoon. I just got off the phone with Aunt Carol. The Queen Bee was rushed to the hospital last night. She had forgotten to take her insulin and passed out. Aunt Carol knew something wasn't right when she called her over and over and got no answer.

We've been getting scares like this the past few months, and Aunt Carol keeps popping in and essentially saving my mother's life. We've all been trying to convince her to move out of her apartment and live someplace where she can be monitored, but she won't budge. She loves her apartment and her independence and wants to do things her way, of course.

I'm not sure what's next. All I know is, you're sitting outside thoroughly enjoying your cookie, kicking your legs up and down off the deck, while I sit at the kitchen table in tears. I haven't been able to talk to my mom yet because she's been busy having so many tests done at the hospital. Aunt Sha spoke to her a few minutes ago and reported that Grandma Buba was yelling at the nurses, "Why do I need all these people? All these questions. Just leave me alone and get outta here, all of you! And take the juice and stale crackers with you. They're full of salt!" Aunt Sha said they're kicking her out of the hospital tomorrow.

I guess she's okay.

Hollyhock

Botanical name: *Alcea rosea*
Family: Malvaceae
"Whaaa-whaa" rating: 4

Hollyhocks were one of the earliest imports to America by the colonists. Known as a medicinal plant, the remains of hollyhocks were found in a fifty-thousand-year-old grave of a Neanderthal man. This plant is the true standby of cottage gardens. They require full sun and regular water but can withstand poor soil. Big, rough, round leaves grow on thick proud stalks, sometimes growing to nine feet tall with 3-6 inch spectacular flowers of white, pink, purple, yellow or apricot. I would have rated this flower a 10, but it is prone to rust, so takes a bit of care. After springtime bloom cut back almost to the ground and you will have another bloom in the fall.
The beautiful round seedpods and generous amount of seeds it leaves for the gardener each fall is unmatched. It took me a few years to grow the first plant by seed. Keep trying. It will come and then keep spreading. Well worth the wait by impatient gardeners and hollyhock addicts.

MAY

Drama Queens

Dear Jack,

We spent the afternoon with our friends Elissa and Joel. We were planning on going to the park, but it turned into one of those foggy freezing San Francisco so-called spring days, so we stayed indoors and turned the heat on high in her living room. We made Peet's coffee and begged her son, Joel, and you to go in the other room and play with puzzles so we could have an uninterrupted conversation. Fat chance. The two of you were either fighting or crying every five minutes. Lucky for us, it began raining and the two of you became fascinated with watching the raindrops fall outside the living room window.

After an in-depth discussion of who makes the best brown lipstick, we somehow segued into the horribly profound topic of losing our parents. It seems lately that all of our friends are beginning to lose a parent. It has become a trend. Elissa's dad recently died unexpectedly of a heart attack. She told me a story about her first day at nursery school. She and her dad were waiting at the bus stop in front of her childhood home. She was crying, frozen with fear when the bus came, so her father, Joe Pinelli—unshaven and dressed in an undershirt, slacks and slippers—shuffled up on the school bus, holding her hand tightly, and accompanied her to her classroom. I had only met her dad once, but I will forever think fondly of the man who rode a New Jersey school bus to take his youngest daughter to school and then quietly walked the half mile back home in his slippers.

❧ ❧

I couldn't attend the Master Gardener graduation this week because I was working. The classes were informative and fun and I miss them already. I've become a more organic gardener. I may have even become a more patient gardener—the jury's still out on that one.

I was working on another spooky and stupid shoot. It was a simple soda commercial that grew more and more daunting as the day progressed. We ended up filming until midnight because the client didn't like the way the *foam* looked in the glass. He made us do thirty-seven takes of the pouring product shot and then decided he didn't like the way the *glass* was lit. So we relit the set at ten o'clock at night and then shot forty more takes. The only thing that kept me awake was watching the squinty-eyed expression on the tired Hell's-Angel-looking prop guy's face. He looked like he was hatching an evil plan to slash the client's tires in the crew parking lot, and pour soda at the same time.

Driving home at one in the morning, a policeman stopped me for going too slow. I'm the only person on the planet who gets stopped for driving too slow. I fear if I drive like an old lady now, how will I drive when I really am an old lady? Will I just be a sitting target? Or will I drive like my grandpa Max, slow and completely oblivious that he was surrounded by raging motorists on Florida's freeways swearing at him.

I spent five minutes explaining the absurdity of the film business to Officer Bob and how my day started at seven this morning. Instead of letting me go home to get some sleep, Officer Bob asked how he could get work as an *extra*. I was so tired that I began wondering if this was really happening or if I was hallucinating. After making me promise to open all the windows and blast the radio to stay awake, he finally let me go. As I drove away, he said, "Drive carefully, Queen Bee." I looked down at my sweater and realized that the tape from my walkie-talkie labeled "Queen Bee" was stuck on my sweater, thanks to my assistant Damon.

For the rest of the drive home, Officer Bob's police car was close behind mine. I was in such a state of exhaustion that every few minutes I changed my mind about him. One minute I decided that I was the most loved Queen Bee in the world, and Bob the nice policeman was making sure I was getting home safely. What a great guy! The next minute I decided that there was something terribly wrong with Bob, maybe he was following me home and he was a little *strange*. Who else would want to be an extra?

The next morning I called my mother to tell her that my crew is now referring to me as the Queen Bee. She said, "I'm proud of you, Mouse. You must be doing a good job." I told her about my drive home. She yelled at me for talking so long to Officer Bob. She's convinced something's wrong with him and that I should've called the police.

"But, Ma, he *is* the police. . . ."

I just got back from spending Mother's Day in San Diego. Ma was thrilled, as she is every Mother's Day, to be surrounded by her four daughters, bouquets of roses and tons of gratitude and appreciation. Unfortunately, the lovefest only lasted about an hour. Aunt

Sha took us all down with her into the snake pit. She piped in about Ma eating too much pecan pie with whipped cream and vanilla ice cream, after her doctor pleaded with her to stay away from sweets. Thanks, Sha, for raining on our parade! The Queen Bee accused us all of being police and spies. Then she decided to perform one of her classic hits loud enough for all the patrons, cooks and dishwashers in the respectable restaurant to hear: *"Who needs kids?!"*

Aunt Sha grabbed you and Cousin Rebecca and left in a huff. Aunt Carol threw some cash on the table and followed. Aunt Augusta, in her best flight attendant voice, asked the Queen Bee, "More coffee?" She got slam-dunked with, "Look how she's starting with me?" So she quickly offered to drive my other sisters home. I could just imagine her on Aunt Sha's cell phone driving and calling the airlines to see if there was an early flight back home to Alabama.

As usual, I was the last one to leave the restaurant because I felt sorry for my mother and, somewhere deep inside, I always thought I could save her. I know I should've been trying to save myself, but, when it came to the Queen Bee, I was clueless. I don't know if it was loyalty, love or just big fat codependence, but I stayed.

To cheer her up, I pulled out an article I had brought with me. It showed a calculation that Edelman Financial Services had made in 1997 estimating that a family would pay $508,700 annually, not counting retirement, health and other benefits, to cover all the jobs a mother does. They came to this amount by adding up the annual salaries of the seventeen occupations a mother is expected to perform.

Didn't the Emancipation Proclamation outlaw slavery over a hundred years ago?

The article also stated that statistically, even when both parents are working outside the home, men contribute only 30 percent of the child-care and domestic duties in the home. *Why are they only giving 30 percent? Weren't they 50 percent responsible for making those babies? (Aren't they supposed to be good in math?)*

We read the article together and she ate up every word of it. We ordered more coffee and discussed the unfairness of it all. She didn't understand how America, a modern nation, where politicians on TV constantly cry fake tears about family values, still treat mothers like second-class citizens. When my parents first met, my dad was in graduate school and Ma was a top hairstylist at the trendy Helena Rubinstein Salon in New York City. When they married, she quit her paid job and worked at home raising her four girls. Twenty-something years later, her life is shattered and she's getting a divorce. The courts wonder what she's been doing for the past twenty years? The saintly duty of raising children isn't considered "real work" because there is no monetary value to it. They tell her to go get a *real* job, at fifty years old. After all the work she put in bringing up the next generation and supporting her husband's career goals, she is now living close to the poverty level. My mother is one of the lucky women who had a compassionate ex-husband who continued giving her alimony long after the courts told him he didn't have to. After all that she has accomplished, she has joined the club of overworked, unhealthy and exhausted divorced, single mothers who are not entitled to any of their ex-husband's social security. They are statistically the poorest old people in the country.

The article ended with, "Most women with dependent children experience a 73 percent drop in standard of living after a divorce, while their ex-husbands' living standard goes up by 42 percent."

My mother looked at me, shaking her head and remarked, "Mouse, your generation of women is educated and you better start believing in yourselves and stop being afraid to ask for what you deserve. You should all be voting for women. What do those old, half-dead men in the senate know about raising kids? Enough! Get them out of there. You want to change the world? Then open your mouth and ask for what you want. Don't just stand there like a statue!"

"Ma, you are the bomb!"

"I am? . . . Is that good?"

Just got off the phone with Aunt Carol. She called today because she and Scott had just watched an episode of *The X-Files* in which these people had a virus that made them keep moving. If they stopped, their heads would blow up.

She said this reminded her of you.

There I was, minding my own business, trying to look like I knew what I was doing at the Master Gardener's desk, and in came Chatty Cathy. She told me that fate has brought us together! The good news was that she had a bag full of rudbeckia seedlings from her garden. The bad news was that I had to listen to a long story about her cat. (Now I know how bored people must be when I tell stories about how funny you are. And then to write a book about you. . . .) Her cat likes to play in the catnip plant. Isn't that fascinating? So I listened to the entire story and she thought I loved cats. I don't love cats. I love dogs. I just put up with cats because they're less work. The whole time I was thinking, "Chatty Cathy, just hand over the goods and leave me alone. Girl, fork over those seedlings!" Thank God the phone rang and I had to answer a question about lawns, my least favorite topic. As she was exiting she said in a frightening, chipper, Kathy-Bates-in-*Misery* voice, "Oh, Annie, we're going to be friends for a long time."

Soon after, I left to go pick you up from Pat's house and we went to the park. As we climbed up the big slide, I hit my head really hard on the steel jungle gym pole and began crying. Of course, you being the whirling dervish you are, just ignored me and carried on in your nonstop way, climbing around, out of control, without one iota of fear. I tried to turn my head to watch you but it hurt too much, so I just lay down on the grass for a few minutes and prayed that nothing would happen to you while I took five minutes off. I was sure I'd been cursed by Chatty Cathy for not paying attention to her stupid cat story. Maybe Papa was right. She's hexed us. Papa said the first time he met her, he heard the music to *Psycho* playing in his head and his left shoulder went into spasm.

Here is why you shouldn't hang up on your mother, ever. I called Grandma Buba at 8:00 A.M. this morning. I was supposed to call her last night to finish a conversation we'd been having, but after hitting my head in the playground, I came home with a splitting "Chatty-Cathy-induced" migraine headache and went to bed early. The only thing I remember about last night was lying there with an ice pack on my head and you demanding me to sing "Louise" to you. Luckily Papa came home from work early so I had to sing it to you only three and a half times.

Well, the Queen Bee yelled at me this morning for not calling her back last night. I tried to explain what a migraine felt like and how you can't talk to anyone, especially *her*, for hours; she didn't think that was a good excuse and hung up on me. Or maybe I hung up on her. It happened so fast that I'm not sure whose turn it was to hang up.

It's two hours later and Aunt Carol just called to say that our mother is in the emergency room and in shock. She is about to be transferred to the burn unit. She fell onto the floor in her bedroom and was blacked out for almost an hour with her arm leaning on the radiator. The paramedics, who saved her life, were trying to figure out how long she had been passed out. The only clue they had was her journal sitting wide open on the dining room table with the last entry being: "8:00 A.M. Just spoke to my daughter on the phone. She was snippy."

They asked Aunt Carol if she was the *snippy* daughter. She said, "Well . . . there are four daughters, and we all have snippy potential when we're talking to our mother. It's called survival. I'll call my sisters and get back to you." So after Aunt Sha and Aunt Augusta played all innocent and goody-goody on the phone, Aunt Carol called and accused me of upsetting the Queen Bee.

Jack, I'm so afraid. I couldn't live with myself if something bad happens to my mother because of me. I admit that once many years ago, when she was visiting, we had our usual fight about why I didn't have any Sweet'n Low in the house and I had a teeny tiny little daydream about her getting stung by a killer bee in my garden.

I've always been the mushy, goody-two-shoes in the family, and now I'll be known as the one who killed her mother by being "snippy."

Last night was the annual Master Gardeners meeting. I arrived early and walked around the garden lit by small white Christmas lights. I thought about my mother, I have been thinking about her nonstop for days. The thought of her in the hospital scares me so much. I spoke to Aunt Carol many times today. The good news is that I didn't kill my mother by being snippy, and she's going to get better. Also, we discovered that there are cute young doctors in the burn unit.

Who knew?

After many years of very dramatic mother-daughter fights, Aunt Carol has now become the picture-perfect daughter. She calls her mother at least twice a day and now the two drama queens are best friends. This is the fifth time that Aunt Carol has saved our mother's life. This time Ma had taken too much insulin, went into shock, fell down near the floor radiator and ended up with third-degree burns all the way up her left arm.

Aunt Carol had been phoning her over the course of an hour or two from work that morning. Unable to get an answer, she called the building manager to go in and check on her. He immediately called 911. When the paramedics got to her, her blood sugar level was at twelve and her heart rate was at twenty-five. (A normal blood sugar level is 70 to 110 ml/dl and a normal heart rate is 72 beats per minute.) It's pretty much a miracle she's alive. Aunt Carol did manage to ask her if she remembered speaking to me on the phone. Grandma Buba said, "Yes, sure I remember talking to Annie. She had nothing to do with this. I'm used to her being snippy. Big deal. So what?"

I went inside to the meeting and it was like a feast. There were tables filled with gourmet dishes and elaborate desserts home-made by Master Gardeners that looked like something only Martha Stewart or Charlie could produce. I had come straight from work. I was supposed to bring cheese and crackers, but since I'd had such a lousy day on the set, I was in the mood for a cold beer. I'd stopped at the supermarket and picked up a case. When I walked into the meeting, the festivities were in full swing. One of the eighty-year-old retired Master Gardeners came running to the door to help me carry the case of beer. He said, "Annie, you're my kind of woman!" Then he asked me to marry him. Before I could respond and even possibly commit, he ran off into the kitchen to hang out with the guys and pop open beer bottles. How can an eighty-year-old man *still* run away from commitment? Grow up!

After half a beer and a glass of red wine, lots of incredible food and some good gossip, I spent the rest of the evening chasing the lady who adds up our volunteer hours and gives us our Master Gardener credits. Cleanup after an event was an easy way to obtain credits. So I followed her around, folding chair after chair and straightening up the room really loudly. I tried to make her notice me, but she kept talking with her lady friends about her yucca plant, while I passed right in front of her nose carrying a stack of twelve folding chairs. When I made it alive to the backroom closet, all twelve chairs fell and made a horrendous crash. Do you think she stopped for one minute? Do you think she cared if I was okay? Nope. She kept on talking about her yucca plant. What is so great about a yucca plant anyway? That's like having a Pekingese.

So I just left.

Ce'cile Brunner
Botanical name: *Rosa rehderiana*
Family: Rosaceae (climbing polyantha)
"Whaaa-whaa" rating: 1

Introduced in 1881, the Ce'cile Brunner, also called the
Sweetheart Rose, has been rated a 7.6 by the American Rose
Society. It is an outstanding climbing polyantha rose. When in
full bloom, it seems to carry you back in time. In only three
years our climber spread over ten feet along the front fence and
continues to grow at a rapid pace. A sun-loving, very healthy
and resilient rose to choose for covering a fence or wall.
Prolific blooms in springtime with sweetly scented,
perfect tiny roses.

JUNE

"I'll Be with You When the Sky is Full of Colors"

Dear Jack,

Yesterday you and I flew to San Diego to join your aunts in packing up the Queen Bee's apartment and moving her into a retirement home, where she will have twenty-four-hour-a-day supervision. We're at her apartment now. Aunt Sha took you and Rebecca down to the playground. You were starting to pull everything out of the boxes we had just filled up with kitchen-wares, clothes, books and Grandma Buba's notebooks. Aunt Carol went back to work for the remainder of the afternoon but left us a big fat list of chores to get done. She thinks she can boss us around just because she saved our mother's life, again. Control freak! Aunt Augusta and I are here, emotionally worn out, packing up Grandma's bedroom drawers.

Whenever I remove a picture from her dresser to pack it, I sit and stare at it for a long time, feeling both empty and over-whelmed. There's the sepia-toned photograph of her when she was twenty-five, glamorous and full of life. Wearing a stylish, 1950s bathing suit, she was flirtatiously posing on the living room floor. Grandpa, who had taken the photograph, must have thought at that moment that he was the world's luckiest guy. There is also our all-time favorite picture of my sisters and me when we were babies.

Grandpa had propped the four of us up on Augusta's bed. We were wearing our lacy dresses and sitting among fluffy white pillows and old-fashioned dolls. Aunt Carol and I were less than a year old. We were so small and sweet, it was hard at first glance to distinguish us from the dolls.

After a long period of silence I realized Aunt Augusta and I had retreated into our own worlds. We had stopped talking. This process of wrapping up our mother's life is too painful for us. At first it was fun to find all the things she had saved from our childhood: letters, birthday cards, black and white photographs, report cards, long-forgotten notes and God-awful children's drawings. But the hard reality has started to set in that our mother is getting old, which means we must be aging too. Time is tapping us on the back, insisting we grow up, but today I feel just as vulnerable as that little girl in the photograph.

Grandma Buba's journal was lying on the dresser next to the shrine of framed pictures of your cousin Rebecca and you. I was curious to see what she had written and began thumbing through it, looking for some dirt on my sisters. Usually she writes which daughter has called and which one hasn't and is therefore in deep trouble or presumed to be in serious straits. Instead, I found on every single journal page the same date and, in her own distinctive handwriting, the same cryptic message written over and over: "I'll be with you when the sky is full of colors." I frantically flipped page after page, feeling lightheaded and sick to my stomach. I shouted to Augusta. We looked at the journal together feeling like we had seen a ghost and found gold at the same time. We were terrified and fascinated. We sat on the bed and tried to analyze what our mother had been trying to say. Maybe it was the insulin, maybe it was her medication or maybe she was just being poetic. She once told Augusta that she writes in her journal to practice her handwriting. We accepted that as the answer because we were too afraid to think of what was really happening.

Feeling drained and confused, we both went back to packing. I emptied the silk scarves and jewelry drawer, thinking it would be a "happy," colorful job, and I was right. My mother had a drawer full of chiffon scarves. I chose a white one with faded pastel flowers on it to keep for myself. I tied it around my head and was sitting there sobbing, when you and Rebecca came back from the park. You didn't notice for one second that I was sad; instead, the two of you jumped right into the scarf drawer and began pulling out colored scarves and wrapping them around your heads. I helped dress you and Rebecca up in jewelry, scarves and the Queen Bee's fancy high heels.

The two of you proudly pranced around the apartment, while I tried to throw away old useless items without Aunt Augusta catching me. Every time I successfully collected a garbage bag full of throwaway items, she'd come in and start digging through it, saving everything. I'd yell, "Why are you saving all this junk?" She'd yell back, "Why are you throwing away all this good stuff?" I'd reply, "Like a blank pocket calendar from 1979, or a rusty old Eiffel Tower key chain with a broken clasp or a cracked Hilton Hotel teacup? That's really useful!" We'd negotiate for a few minutes. She confused me so that somehow I ended up keeping the broken Eiffel Tower key chain because I knew how much my mother loved Paris. Then we'd go our separate ways and begin the whole throwing away–keeping things process over again.

When Aunt Sha came to help, we secretly became a team. Aunt Sha, of course, has not one iota of patience, so she'd shuffle through a drawer for two minutes, then pull the drawer out, dump the remaining contents into a garbage bag, tie it up and toss it into the hallway. She and I began hiding garbage bags full of junk in the hallway closet. When Aunt Augusta was in the other room, I'd shove them into Aunt Sha's arms and push her out the door, so she'd get to the alley Dumpster before Augusta came back into the room. We were under the gun to finish the packing today and Augusta was slowing down the production line. She was about to be fired from the project by bossy I-don't-have-time-for-this Aunt Sha!

Tomorrow we'll be moving everything into the retirement home and taking shifts visiting Grandma Buba at the hospital. Aunt Carol had us working around the clock—recrimination for her being our mother's caretaker for the past few years. How she stays so resilient and loyal to the Queen Bee, I'll never know.

In the middle of this messy, emotional, power-packing operation, Grandpa arrived. His immediate and primary concern was why you were walking around wearing a necklace and high heels. He stripped you of your very fashionable accessories and took you two pipsqueaks out for ice cream.

We just got back from the hospital. The Queen Bee is doing amazingly well. She's sharp as a tack. Aunt Carol got there before we worker bees did. She had put makeup and a colorful scarf on Grandma Buba to make her look festive. When we entered the room, the party began. We were celebrating Augusta's birthday! While you and Rebecca fought over who should carry the "Over the Hill" balloon, Grandma Buba recognized and admired all her jewelry and scarves that we had on. She said she was glad we were wearing them. We sang happy birthday to Augusta and ate cupcakes. Of course, you had to touch every piece of sterile medical equipment in the room. Then you'd press all the buttons on

Grandma Buba's bed, making her head and feet fly up in the air. Then you'd roughly climb up on top of her burned bandaged arm to sit next to her. I kept waiting for her to scream at you but instead she just hugged and kissed you.

We kept singing and laughing—all of us perfectly happy to stay in sweet denial. No one dared mention the topic of the impending burn surgery. Everything was fine and dandy for a while, and then you stunk up the room with a nasty diaper. At the same time, the Queen Bee, with one very weak and crispy arm, still managed to toss in a jab or two. She looked at the rest of us and asked about Augusta, as if she weren't sitting right there, "Why can't she wear lipstick on her birthday? Would it kill her to wear some lipstick?" We sat silently. After all these years, one thing we've learned is that if you can't agree with her, don't reply at all. So we all just stared at the walls and hummed to ourselves. Then she looked at me and snapped, "Why do you let him touch everything? This place is full of germs. That kid has ants in his pants. Make him stop moving. Phew. What stinks?" Aunt Sha must've known she was the next target, so she quickly started saying good-bye. We left, pleased with the notion that it was a good sign that our mother still had it in her to torture us.

Have I told you about Dr. Joe? He's Grandma Buba's cute burn surgeon. He came into her room early this morning to explain the surgical procedure and the recovery time frame. Aunt Carol and I simultaneously melted into his eyes, as he compassionately advised us on how to take care of our mother as she heals from burn surgery. When he turned away from us to talk to Grandma Buba, I whispered to Aunt Carol, "He is too cute!" She shushed me and went on to asking more questions about the surgery. The two of them spoke for way too long in medical jargon, which Aunt Carol understands being a doctor herself, and left me to stew in sibling rivalry. When Dr. Joe left the room, Aunt Carol looked at me and said, "He was definitely flirting with me. I mean, wasn't he? I'm sure he was. Wasn't he?" I rolled my eyes, became twelve years old and full of jealousy and said, "Was not." Then we turned around to say good-bye and good luck to our mom. With her eyes half closed and looking drowsy from the presurgery medication, she had a big smile on her face and her shoulders were shaking under the blanket.

She was laughing at us.

It's been an agonizing week. All of your loud, irrepressible aunts are left scared, overwhelmed and exhausted. As I write this, Grandma Buba is in her second and most difficult burn surgery. I won't go into the gruesome details of skin grafting, because it's horrific. She will be in recovery for a week and then we will move her into the retirement home. Every time we drop off a car full of her belongings to her new home, I feel a pit in the bottom of my stomach. I didn't think this day would come so soon.

We are back home. Today is Aunt Sha's birthday. We called her early this morning. You wouldn't sing "Happy Birthday" to her, so she sang it to you. This morning you helped me fertilize the garden with fish emulsion and seaweed. Then we deadheaded the roses. Two weeks from now, we'll feed the roses with Epsom salt. You have become almost helpful out there. At least you're trying. You follow me around, saying, "Helping, helping." So I give you a watering can and you spill it all over yourself.

Today you discovered the cherry tree. You stood there for about twenty minutes, eating every single ripe cherry off the lower branches. You'd point to the higher branches and say, "Upstairs. " I told you we had to save those for Papa and you got all upset. You went and sat in the puddle of water you made on the deck with your watering can and moped. That didn't get my attention, so you began swatting the rose bushes with your plastic shovel, and that made me mad. Not even two years old and you already know how to push my buttons. Amazing.

While working in the garden this afternoon, I had some vivid childhood memories in which I saw my mother in full color and heard her voice . . . let's just say, a little too well. It was winter 1973 in Manhattan. I was fourteen years old. My sisters and I were in our dining room, eating supper dressed in down vests, mittens and ear muffs. We intentionally dressed like this to aggravate our mother, who always needed "air." Even in a blizzard she had all the windows flung open, with curtains blowing and a winter wonderland forming in our apartment.

Our father had just phoned from Europe, where he was on another business trip. They had recently been separated. His phone calls, though warm and loving to us, put my mother in a spin. She existed in a combustible state already, and his calls would set her off.

"There he is gallivanting around the world on fancy business trips and I'm stuck here with four snippy kids, cooking and cleaning and dying of loneliness. Don't you dare ever do this! Don't be stupid. Don't you ever become dependent on anyone. Don't become a prisoner. Get your education. Make your own money, your own career. Who needs kids? *Who needs men?* Open the windows! *I need AIR!"*

"Stop hitting me with your elbow! Get your mitten out of my soup!" Carol snipped at me.

Augusta said calmly, "Ma, those are some valid positions you made and we respect your opinion, but I think it's not appropriate dinner conversation."

I mumbled inside my wool scarf, "And we've seen this show about fifty times too many. We've memorized every word, and not by choice."

Then the kicker, Sha yelled loudly, *"And we are freezing. Every window is wide open! There is a snowstorm outside and there are no more windows to open! . . . Are you crazy?"*

And with that we were all kicked out of the house with our golden wonder dog, Fluffy, who as he exited barked and growled at our mother one last time, before she slammed the door.

The Queen Bee has been in her new retirement home for three days, and she swears she hasn't yelled at anyone yet. She told me that when she left the hospital, all four nurses scurried around her wheel-chair, kissing and hugging her good-bye. They told her how much they would miss her. I immediately called Aunt Carol to see if that was true or imagined. She says it's true. We can't quite figure it out. She had charmed her way into their hearts! We think that maybe after two weeks of being around our mother, these nurses got used to her yelling at them one moment and then telling them how smart and beautiful they were the next. Aunt Carol and I deduced that these four nurses were just as codependent as the rest of us.

Well, the Queen Bee has done it again: managed to alienate the entire staff at her retirement home in just ten days. Dolores, one of the big shots in charge, said in her Southern drawl, "Why, I have never been treated so rudely in my whole life!" After Dolores exited Grandma Buba's room, the Queen Bee looked at Aunt Carol and said, "Keep her outta here and all the other ones too. All day long in and out, in and out. They're wearing out the carpet! Get rid of them all. They're getting on my nerves. I want to be left alone."

Translated, this means that she wants to be left alone to call Carol five times a day, every time she needs something big or small. Yesterday she needed a needle for sewing, today she needed a battery for the TV remote. (Which was working fine—she was just pressing "off" instead of "on.") Tomorrow who knows what she'll need, but you can bet Carol will hear about it.

Speaking of demanding people, I took you to the Magic Garden Nursery in Berkeley today. I was looking forward to a tranquil nursery visit and instead you went ballistic. You refused to sit in your stroller. You had to push it yourself. If I let you push it, you'd run over people and plants, and crash into exotic pottery. So I had to strap you into it, which you detest. You began wailing and I started getting dirty looks from those lucky, child-free, happy gardeners, all wondering, I'm sure, why anyone would bring a screaming child to such a tranquil place. As you were crying, I ran out of there, trying to look in control of the situation, crossing bumpy gravel pathways that made pushing an old rickety hand-me-down stroller almost impossible.

GROWING SEASONS

Two high points of my day:
1. When you took your nap.
2. When you fell asleep for the night.

Just completed a busy afternoon shift at the Master Gardener desk. I was very lucky to have David, the arborist, working with me, because I know so very little about trees. We had four on-the-verge-of-annoying people come in with specific questions about their oak, quince and ironwood trees. I tried to look interested while David diagnosed each one of them perfectly. Then our boss-lady, Effie, helped me find the arborist manual so we could make more specific suggestions. I double-checked David's theories with Pavel Svihra, our horticulture advisor, who is a walking plant encyclopedia and then phoned back the people and recited our suggestions and solutions, as if I had come up with them on my own. I took all the credit for giving them the correct answers. David, in his great Mississippi drawl, said it didn't surprise him one bit that I took all the credit, since I was from New York.

Once the phone calls slowed down, I had some time to work on *my* garden issues . . . finally. I sketched a plan for the front lawn. I want to add a path with steppingstones. This would make the lawn smaller, and maybe I could learn to like the lawn. I came home and showed my idea to Papa. He hated the whole thing. He said it wouldn't work. We argued. In the end he said, *"Fine.* It's your project. I don't want anything to do with your harebrained idea." I snapped back that I didn't care what "Mr. Man" said and that I was going to do it without his help.

The only problem is I kinda-sorta need his help.

Poisonous spiders often live together amicably, but if a black widow happens to be hungry, she will sometimes eat her mate for supper.

If only it were that simple. . . .

I'm writing to you while sitting in a tent overlooking the Yuba River outside the town of Sierraville. Your papa and I came up to the mountains to camp here for his birthday weekend. You are staying with the wonderful disciplinarian, Grandma Gin-Gin. We'll see you tonight. We talk incessantly about how much we miss you and then, practically in the same sentence, talk about how fun it is to not be in "parent" mode.

We saw so many stars last night. We made a campfire and Papa pointed out the North Star, the Big Dipper and some of the more obvious constellations to me. It's hard for me to distinguish the constellations. In New York I would rarely see the stars because of the city's bright lights. Plus, my mother had ingrained in us from childhood that if you were out somewhere where it was dark enough to actually see stars, it surely must be a dangerous place, and you should immediately search out "normal" people and call for help.

We borrowed Betty's raft yesterday afternoon and went rafting for three hours at Snag Lake. We had the whole lake to ourselves. (That's only because Papa made us drag the raft two miles by foot through the woods to find the most deserted section of the lake. Okay, maybe it was just a couple hundred feet. Whatever the distance was, it was treacherous, grueling and extremely dangerous, and if there were any people around, you can bet they weren't "normal.")

The day was clear and sunny with the perfect amount of cool summer breeze to keep us comfortable and not too hot. We laughed at the thought of you being with us. You would've been demanding to row the boat saying, "Jack's turn" a hundred times until Papa and I were miserable and not talking to each other anymore. Instead, we had a cooler full of sandwiches and drinks, *Fine Gardening* and *Outside* magazines, sun hats and Trader Joe's Coffee candies. We were having the time of our lives! When we got to the center of the lake, we put our feet up on the side of the boat and hung out in the sun, telling each other stories. Papa tried to explain to me what was so great about the Jeffrey pine trees surrounding the lake. I said, "I just don't get it. They look like all the other Christmas trees in the world." He said, "That's because you're turning into the Queen Bee. Can't you just hear her? Uch, what's with all these trees? This is where the cult leaders live—here in the woods. Enough with the woods!"

Guess what? Aunt Carol and Uncle Scott are going to have a baby! She is pregnant and we are all so thrilled. We were a little concerned that she wouldn't get pregnant, because she doesn't really have time to have a baby. She has long difficult hours at work, goes out dancing at night and has a demanding mother to take care of. But somehow she managed to fit in having a baby. She never ceases to amaze me.

Watch her turn out to be a nauseatingly happy new mother just like Aunt Sha was with Cousin Rebecca. I stopped phoning Sha back then because each time I did she'd say, "Annie, I'm so in love with her. I want to have four more babies! No, five more! Okay, well, no more than six!"

And I'd say, "That's nice Sha . . . I have to go now." Then I'd pray to the heavens to please give me back my raspy, loud and impatient big sister from those scary baby people who put a Marie Osmond spell on her. I had to save her! I stopped calling her, but she'd leave me messages on my answering machine with the sounds of Baby Rebecca sweetly cooing.

As a last resort, I'd call the Queen Bee and say, "Ma, can you believe Sha wants to have five more babies? Don't you find that a little sickening? I mean . . . why?"

"So she wants six kids. Why is it your business? Leave her alone. She's happy. What are you, the police?"

"Ma, I think she's joined a very frightening cult. We need to get her back. You need to talk some sense into her. Someone has to stop her. *She's freaking me out, Ma!*"

"Uch, stop with the nonsense. I'm watching *Jerry Springer.*"

Click.

❧ ❧

Well, I might hate the harebrained lawn idea after all. I'm not sure yet. I was trying to do it organically, but I think I'm going to have to get out the big guns. There's too much Bermuda grass to cover. I was going to add wood chips and steppingstones without laying any fabric underneath. But the Bermuda grass is so invasive that I'm going to have to use Round-Up and fabric before placing the stones, as your papa suggested.

So what if he was right. Big deal.

He finally decided he'd help me with my project. He didn't seem very happy about it. He said I sucker-punched him into helping me by looking so pitiful. He also threatened to never ever let me forget this crackpot idea of mine. I'm relieved he'll help because he'll do excellent and thorough work. But you can bet he'll be miserable and I'll hear about it. And when it's all done, I can take credit for how good it looks because it was my idea.

And that's how marriage works!

This evening I set out snail bait around the tomatoes and sunflowers. I'm trying beer. Supposedly a couple of saucers full will do the trick. Bud and Michelob are the preferred brands. The snails are attracted to the yeast. Snails and slugs are hermaphrodites. This is pure proof that the world is very unfair and that Mother Nature must have been so overwhelmed some days with motherhood that she went a little berserk. Hermaphrodites have the reproductive capabilities of both sexes. *Six* times a year a slug or snail will hide eighty eggs under the topsoil.

I know. What's the use?

Poppy
Botanical name: *Papaver*
Family: Papaveraceae
"Whaaa-whaa" rating: 1

One of the few flowers that actually reseeds in our garden is
the poppy. Charlie gave us some seeds a few years back and
now, magically, Shirley poppies *(Papaver rhoeas)* and Oriental
poppies *(Papaver orientale)* come up each summer all over the
garden. Each year they seem to double and spread their
gorgeous red and orange paperlike flowers all around our
property. Poppies enjoy full sun and little water. When the
stems turn brown, break off the outstanding capsules and
remove thousands of seeds to lightly rake into the soil the
following early spring. Some poppies do well as cut flowers.
The night before you think a poppy will open, dip the cut end
into boiling water for thirty seconds.

Annie's recommendation: Shop at Annie's Annuals
(no relation) on-line for a superlative selection of rare poppies.

JULY

The Egos Have Landed

Dear Jack,

The little harebrained idea has grown and taken on a life of its own. Actually, it's become gargantuan and I wouldn't blame Papa if he never spoke to me again. He is out there remeasuring everything that I estimated. My measurements were way off. I used my footsteps instead of a tape measure. I'm afraid to tell him . . . but somehow he must know, because he's giving me dirty looks and shaking his head a lot. There are some people who measure and others who "ballpark." I'm a ballparker. I'd never hire *me* to build anything. It's close to 98 degrees and he has a little bit of leftover flu bug that you so kindly brought home. He's out in the hot sun looking like he's going to faint and kill me at the same time. I keep saying, "Babe, we can make this *fun*. I promise. We can learn to enjoy working together." He doesn't answer me, and I can't think of any way to make this *fun*.

We're close to halfway done with the job. It looks good but it's been a horrible experience. Some projects look so simple, but once you get started, they seem to grow and grow. The best part of the whole crackpot idea is the beautiful birdbath we bought and placed right in the center of the lawn.

I hate to say it, but maybe that's all it needed in the first place.

In the evening we took you to the lake to watch your first fireworks display. You were absolutely fascinated with them. We sat along the lake with hundreds of picnickers and lawn chair warriors—big and small, all intrigued with the sky full of colors. I held you in my arms, wrapped in a blanket. I watched you and Papa watching the fireworks with the same sparkle in your eyes and smiles on your faces, and I felt really lucky.

I'm sitting here in the sun trying to erase from my mind the awful commercial I have been working on the past few days. The female director was cold, calculating, phony and evil—and that is sugar-coating it. Papa now refers her to as "The Little Ball of Hate." We were location-scouting in the van the first day when I overheard her telling the prop guy that she was a very "spiritual" person. I shoved open the window next to me so I could get some fresh air. I felt like I was going to get sick. She's officially excommunicated from the sisterhood. She got worse and worse with each day on the shoot, and I lost any hope of practicing nonjudgment.

Yesterday we were filming at a farm with a magnificent view of the hills that made you feel as if you were in a Dick and Jane storybook, so pure and sweet. We arrived at the set just in time to witness a spectacular sunrise over the hills. Then I heard a car door slam. The egos had landed. The Little Ball of Hate had arrived in her convertible Mercedes. I went over to her and her entourage for an update on some camera equipment and she snarled, "Don't ever touch me again."

I thought, convertible Mercedes. *One phone call to New York Mike. Slashed tires by sundown. . . .*

The day could have been a pleasant one. It was actually not a complicated shoot. We had only two actors, a great crew, very few shots to film, and we were there in God's country. However, The Little Ball of Hate had so many satanic spirits spewing out of her, an indication of deep inner conflict, that the set was filled with thick, hot tension all day long.

At sunset all mayhem broke out. We were losing the daylight and the wind was kicking up as we tried to get our last shot. In the middle of the usual magic-hour cinematic chaos, a herd of cows casually strolled up the hill right in the center of her shot. The client yelled over to us that he didn't want the commercial to look "so rural." *(Then why are we shooting on a farm? . . .)* The Little Ball of Hate started yelling at everyone around her, "Get rid of the cows, get rid of the stupid cows!" My wonderful assistant, Damon, was tossed over the fence and forced to get rid of a large, stubborn herd of cows that were just about to settle down and take a nice nap. We were filming the two actors on the side lawn and there in the background is Damon—this loud New Yorker—running around the field with a bullhorn, screaming in a thick, Long Island accent, "Go home, cows, you're in the shot. Get lost. Scram!!" I called on my walkie-talkie for the farmer and his cowboy brother to go help Damon. I wasn't as worried about getting the shot as I was about one of those cows being a bull. The ranch guys were racing toward the hillside when the Little Ball of Hate looked at me and in her condescending tone asked, "Why aren't they running faster? What's taking so long? Why can't *you* get rid of those cows?"

Definitely slashed tires.

Yesterday we took Betty's raft to Tomales Bay to enjoy a day in the sun as a family. Ha! Once we were at the beach and all geared up to head out into the water, we realized that we had lost the air cap to the raft, so we couldn't blow it up. Just then you threw up your scrambled egg breakfast all over me. The windy roads must've made you sick. Frustrated, depressed and smelling like vomit on a beautiful summer day, we drove home. We spent most of the day concocting an elaborate story to tell Betty about her damaged goods, trying to in some way make her the one to blame and calling local dive shops to find replacement parts for her faulty raft.

❧ ❧

Grandpa flew in from New York City this morning. I picked him up at the airport while you and Papa went out for a bike ride. When you saw your grandpa get out of the car, you dashed across the front lawn straight into his arms. The two of you hugged long and hard looking like you couldn't live without each other. He babysat for you this afternoon while you splashed around in your plastic pool. He later told me you said, "No" about twenty times in one hour. Then he asked if you even knew how to say "Yes"? I said you didn't.

At sunset you and I went over to Betty's house to water her tomatoes while she is on vacation. Of course you demanded to be allowed to hold the hose and got me soaking wet in minutes. Every time I tried to take charge of the situation, you'd yell, "No, Mama. You're *naughty!*" So I let you make a big mess while I wandered around Betty's vegetable garden, pondering how it's possible that I am a Master Gardener (and all of my tomatoes are infected with Verticillium wilt), while she is a novice gardener (with absolutely perfect, gorgeous tomatoes)! How embarrassing is that?

We arrived home sopping wet, thanks to you and your I-have-to-do-it-all attitude. I told Papa about Betty's tomato plants. He suggested we dig out her plants while she's away and switch them with our yellow, brown, droopy, pathetic tomato plants. And then, in my most benevolent Master Gardener voice, I should offer to help her with her pitiful vegetable garden.

I actually considered it for a few moments but decided it was way too much work for such a hot afternoon.

Right now I'm writing to you, or trying to write to you, while Papa sits here bothering me. He keeps trying to talk to me, just to distract me. I tell him it's a sin to intentionally aggravate people you love. But he keeps reading aloud to me from *Organic Gardening*. I stop writing for a moment and look at the pictures of beautiful one-year-old gardens, and I want to get down on my knees and weep.

Papa and I then agree on how much we hate the back lawn and how tired we are of watering it. It is an easy target to take out our frustrations on. I drew him a plan I had come up with for the back-yard that would get rid of at least half the lawn. I thought he was going to argue with me, but instead he agreed. Then he diagrammed his plan. I looked and listened to his idea. Not a bad one.

Not as good as mine, but not bad.

I just got off the phone with the Queen Bee. She was watching *Judge Judy*, her favorite TV program.

(Note: This is not a good time to phone.)

"Ma, you sound so good! I'm so happy for you. You sound like you're beginning to like your new home."

"Not particularly." (Pause) "Why do you always put words in

my mouth? First she puts words in my mouth. Then she puts words in my ears. Look what she does to me? Four beautiful daughters I raised and this is what I get. Tsk, tsk, tsk." Click.

Grandpa left this afternoon. It's 8:00 P.M. and you just went to sleep. I'm a bit suspicious that you went down so easily. The past few days you've followed Grandpa around like a little puppy dog. Those little feet of yours never stopped moving. He's probably ready for a real vacation now.

On the way to the airport we made a stop at Green Gulch Farm. It's become an annual trip for us. We sat on a bench in the garden and talked for a while. Then he handed me a gold pocket watch that his grandfather Wolf gave to my grandfather Max, who passed it on to my dad, and he is now passing it on to you. This pocket watch is a bittersweet heirloom. It was given to my father when he was ten years old by his grandfather during the Nazi occupation of Belgium. Many times when they were hiding in fields behind haystacks, barns and trees, escaping the German soldiers, my brave great-grandfather Wolf would grab my dad and whisper, "Pay close attention. When I tell you to run, head for those trees and hide there until someone calls your name. When you hear gunshots, drop to the ground and don't move. The Lord will help us and you will be safe."

Wolf told my father, if they were ever separated, to take the watch to the nearest farmhouse and give it to the residents so that they would take care of him and hide him from the Nazis. Due to the skill and unfathomable courage of my grandparents Max and Rose, along with a little divine intervention, my father and his younger sister, my aunt Ceil, survived several months of hiding out in small villages narrowly evading the Nazi deportations to concentration camps. My dad never had to use the watch and is alive today to pass it on to you. He also told me that more than three hundred members of our immediate family in Europe were not so lucky. After World War II only eighteen relatives were known to have survived. It was truly a family massacre.

I sat there stunned and speechless for a long time.

When I recovered from the story, I walked around the lettuce fields and stared at eight-foot-tall sunflowers, protecting the gold watch in my hand, this little piece of history that lives on.

When I returned to the bench, my dad's eyes were closed, so I sat next to him and closed mine. I thought about you. I thought about how close you are with your grandfather. Earlier today, after I dropped you off at Pat's house, I came home and cleaned up any trace of Grandpa's belongings from your room. While Grandpa packed his bags for his flight, I kept saying to him, "Dad, we have to get Jack's room back to normal before he comes home so he doesn't feel sad," as I was feverishly tossing things into bags and closets. Then when I was sitting on the bench next to him in the garden, I realized it was *me* I was trying to protect from the pain of coming home and finding my dad gone. I was just about to break down in tears and tell him that I couldn't live without him and that he must move to California, when he opened his eyes and started talking about a recipe from Provence he'd seen in the *New York Times*. Something about grilled salmon with mustard sauce and fresh peppercorns.

I said, "Dad, this is so typical. I bring you to a spiritual place and you think about food."

He looked at his watch and said, "Hey, it's almost noon. Are you hungry? I'm getting hungry. Let's go have lunch!"

Last night at 2:00 A.M. I woke up because I heard talking in the kitchen. I stumbled in and found you sitting on your papa's lap, eating a Popsicle and discussing your purple balloon that had "pop-ded." You were wide awake for two hours and your wonderful papa stayed up with you so I could sleep. I had to be on the set at 5:00 A.M. One thing I want you to know when you grow up is how much better your papa was about being up with you in the middle of the night than I. He was always so patient with you. I was not. I was wearily keeping an inner tab on just how many hours of sleep you were depriving me of. Someday when you are a lazy, miserable teenager who hates me and sleeps till noon, I will wake you up at dawn—payback for every single hour you took from me.

Last night Papa was forced to watch *Barney's Campfire* with you at 3:00 A.M. You have no idea what torment that is for "your people." (Yet another thing everyone forgot to mention in the "parenting" job description.) Barney is bad enough in the daytime. I can't even imagine the excruciating pain of 3:00 A.M. Barney! I see major payback ahead for you.

It's 102 degrees outside. Our poor garden looks pitiful. I'm lying beside you on the bed underneath the cool breeze of the ceiling fan. Surrounding us are three red balloons. This morning, on the way home from the store, we passed a used-car lot with balloons attached to the cars for sale. You whaaa-whaa-ed out on me, so I screeched to a stop and, with the car still running and you still wailing, made a total fool of myself by grabbing balloons off of used Toyotas and tossing them into the backseat so we could drive home in peace. And here you are next to me, looking so beautiful as you sleep. I can't resist. I kiss you a few times on the cheek and run my fingers through your long blond hair. You look so innocent. You can't possibly be that same pathological balloon fanatic.

Butterfly Bush

Botanical name: *Buddleja davidii*
Family: Buddlejaceae
"Whaaa-whaa" rating: 2

Named after the Reverend Adam Buddle—a horticultural cleric in Essex, England, who believed that studying plants would bring him closer to understanding God's universe— butterfly bush, sometimes called summer lilac, is a fast-growing, reasonably drought-tolerant, charming shrub that can grow 4-10 feet tall. It has lilac-like spikes of deep purple blossoms and is one of the least demanding shrubs in our yard. It blooms all summer long. After first bloom cut back by a third to encourage late summer bloom.
After the second bloom cut back the entire plant within a few inches of the ground.
Blooms are available in lilac, white, orange or yellow.

AUGUST

The Moon's Behind the Clouds

Dear Jack,

You and I are in San Diego visiting the Queen Bee. Grandpa picked us up at the airport late this afternoon and I've hardly seen you since. You can't bear to have Grandpa out of your sight.

Aunt Carol came home after work with Chinese food and picked up Grandma Buba on the way over. She looked so well and strong for someone who had recently undergone burn surgery. You were relatively well behaved through dinner, then I found you alone in the living room climbing on top of the piano, trying to get to Aunt Carol's only crystal vase that was a wedding present. I got there too late. You marked it with a nice little chip. I'm not exactly sure how you managed to chip it, but Aunt Carol was mad at me for the rest of the visit. She probably thinks I'm the worst mother.

Before I had a child, I always wondered why people let their bratty kids run around like wild banshees. Now I see. You can be the most responsible parent, keeping a sharp eye on your child all day long, and then the one minute you stop to take a deep breath or sit down—or even, more daringly, take a moment for yourself—that's when disaster hits. And that's when everyone who doesn't have children is standing there wondering why you're not in control.

After dinner I drove the Queen Bee back to her retirement

home. I hadn't been there since we moved her in earlier this summer. I was a little hesitant, thinking it would be upsetting, but it was just fine. Aunt Carol decorated the place so nicely that it has a clean, bright feel to it. Grandma Buba sat down in her Queen Bee chair while I went to the ice machine in the hall to get her a glass of water. When I returned, I handed the glass to her filled to the brink with ice, and she said, "It's not cold."

"Ma, it's cold water with ice filled to the top. It's very cold."

"No. It's not cold."

"Ma, I promise you, it's cold."

I thought, This is just like dealing with Jack! *Stay calm. Use distraction.* And it worked! I admired the new nightgowns that Aunt Carol had bought for her. We played dress-up for half an hour. I helped her change into each of them and then, in pure Dysfunctional Family Tradition, we smiled and took pictures and pretended everything was just fine. We decided the pink flowery one was the best and chose that one for tonight's sleep. I helped her undress. I kept staring at her burned arm and the red raw skin on the front of her thighs where the surgeons had taken skin to save her arm. I told her she looked cool, like she's wearing hot pants. We both laughed. But I was thinking to myself, How could they do this to my mother?

When I left her building, I heard her calling, "Annie, Annie," and I turned to see her waving from her ground floor patio door in her beautiful new nightgown with pink tulips on it. "I love you, Mouse," she yelled. I kept walking to the car, waving and smiling and blowing her kisses into the warm summer night. I turned on the headlights knowing she couldn't see my face, watching her watch me, and the tears started falling. I cried so uncontrollably all the way back to Aunt Carol's that I got lost. I didn't notice that I was on the wrong freeway for a long, long time.

Ten more minutes and I would've been in Mexico drinking a Corona with lime.

"He wants blood."

That's what my mother said after spending one long afternoon with you at her new home. (She also said that about the Republicans, who were spending "her money" persecuting Bill Clinton. "They want his blood and then they'll be happy.") You really needed a nap but refused to take one. You were overtired and running nonstop around her small living room, exhausting all of us. You went absolutely berserk when Grandpa went to do some errands without you. You are slightly obsessed with him. You two are quite the pair, sitting around all day having snacks and telling fishing stories, even though I don't think my dad has ever really caught a fish. He tells you all these fabricated fishing tales as the two of you munch on fattening foods that he should not be eating. He says they are for *you*. He now has a partner in crime.

You are finally taking a nap. Aunt Carol and I are sitting in her backyard, relaxing in the sun. We are resting now so we will have our second wind when you wake up. Surrounding me are her abundant tomato plants and tall, citrus trees filled with chunky, beautiful lemons. I'm sitting here giving her a fertilizing schedule but she seems to be doing fine without it. "Everything just grows on its own!" she chirps in her happy-go-lucky way. Can she not see just how bitter I am? I don't think she says it to hurt or impress me. She's just as surprised as I am. It's the effortless way she says it that gets to me. Your papa says he sees right through her, that she is definitely bragging about easy lemons to torment me because my feral child chipped her crystal wedding vase.

Last week, before we left on our trip to Aunt Carol's, Papa and I met with Gregory, a landscape designer, something we should have done about five years ago. We did the whole garden backward. We planted it all and now we're planning it. Brilliant! Gregory came over to give us some ideas on getting rid of the dead back lawn. When he left, Papa looked at me and said, "He didn't even say one nice thing about the garden. Not one little compliment. We must look like novices to him. I'm so embarrassed." We stared at each other and commiserated about all the hard work, time and money we'd put into the yard, and how at certain times and in certain moods, it still resembled trailer-park neglect. We may as well park a boat on the front lawn, add a few fake deer and some gnomes and give up on the cottage-garden idea. We walked around the yard trying to find one area, just one tiny section we could be proud of, where there were happy healthy thriving plants in the right place. The best we could do was the little corner near the fig tree with Papa's Shasta daisies. Daisies. Here I am boasting to Aunt Carol, who is so easily impressed with my botanical skills, and I'm busy growing daisies.

Shasta freaking daisies.

Okay, so maybe it was a harebrained idea after all. And maybe we did it all backward, but it's sure to look really nice soon. I think. Today our neighbor, Mark, came over to help us sod the front lawn. We tilled in fresh new soil and tomorrow we will lay down the sod. Well, I shouldn't really say "we." Papa and Mark did most of the work. Papa hates me today. This front lawn project seems to just keep growing, and the more it grows, the more he glares at me. The more he glares at me, the longer it will take him to forgive me.

Next week Gregory will be here to measure the backyard so he can begin a plan there. I figured out how to have the perfect garden. Work a lot of hours so you can make a lot of money and hire real, live professional landscapers who know what they're doing! That's the ticket. And then you take all the credit for your beautiful garden.

And then you write a book about it.

Aunt Carol just had to tattle to the Queen Bee about the crystal vase you chipped. Your energy seemed to wipe everyone out down there and they're all still recuperating. Grandma Buba says I should send Aunt Carol a check for the chipped vase and . . . put you on a leash.

Today while filming a sunrise shot on Mount Tamalpais, Huey, the talented key grip who could build or rig anything in the world and the father of three teenage girls, informed me of a new club he is starting called WOOF, Women Out of Film. (This imaginary Neanderthal club only exists in his head, and he tells me about it just to start my day off right by annoying me at 5:00 A.M.) He started it because of Jimmy Stewart, a cute grip with the sweetest Arkansas accent who attracts all the women crew members on the set. Jimmy could tell us the most ridiculous joke and we would all laugh because he is so charming. We'd just stand there cooing. Then all the other cute young grips would come over and we'd be socializing at Craft Service, pouring cold sodas and iced tea as if we were at a high school dance instead of lighting the set.

Thus began WOOF.

Is Huey just older, shorter, bitter and jealous? One can only imagine.

Later that night I mentioned WOOF to Mr. Louie on the phone. Mr. Louie has dreamed up his own imaginary club of chauvinistic morons called "MenZ." The club's lone objective is for the MenZ to sit around all day watching sports while being served snacks and beer by their female partners, who are quietly and cheerfully finishing up the household chores. *As if!* Mr. Louie wants to know how he can become a charter member of WOOF. There's a match made in heaven. He thinks maybe this Huey fellow could be a genius or possibly a demigod.

Note: For just a small amount of cold, hard cash, I'd be happy to share Huey's home phone number.

And for a couple of bucks more, I'd toss in Mr. Louie's.

Today you, Papa and I were shopping at REI for cycling gear. We took turns shopping while the other one watched you. I took you over to the tent department and we pretended we were camping, which kept your attention for about five minutes. You were much happier running around the store and hiding behind racks full of fleece and ski wear. This was okay for a moment or two, as long as I knew which rack you were hiding behind. I turned my eyes away from you for a few seconds to look at some hats, and when I looked back you were gone.

I started looking through aisles of clothes' racks calling your name, first calmly and playfully, then beginning to panic, I turned into a wild mother bear smashing through racks and shoppers in my way. Papa heard me from across the store and came running over to help. We each went in a different direction to look for you. I went to camping and he went to climbing. After a few minutes, which felt like hours, I ran to the front register like a madwoman demanding they close all the doors till I found my son. The twenty-year-old-surfer-type manager gave me a look that said, "Chill out, lady." He got on the store paging system, announced a lost child and gave a description of you. "Wild, blond, two-year-old with purple T-shirt lost in store." Then he just went about his business! I wanted to grab the microphone and first beg and then demand that every single person in the store stop what they were doing and *find my son!* I stood on the top stair of the store searching for some moving clothing racks or loose blond hair hiding behind a down coat.

I was close to breaking down in tears. I was thinking to myself: I need a crew. This is all wrong. There should be production assistants locking up the back door. I can't do this on my own. I need my people! Then I came back to my senses and stared at all the shoppers in line, seeing if they were hiding a two-year-old boy under their purchases. Everyone was suspect. None of them seemed to care. *Why doesn't anyone care? Stop shopping, you superficial mass consumers of fleece!*

Then I saw Papa way over in the back of the store searching the boot section. He turned and headed back to me, looking discouraged and angry and without you. I decided when he reached me that we would call the police. Then out of the corner of my eye, accelerating quickly out of the ski department, something flashed. It was a blond, tornado in a purple T-shirt destroying everything in its path with two ski poles, tips pointed right at me, shrieking, *"Charge!!!!!"*

While Papa paid for his bike gear, you and I went to the car. There I found two bells from old balloons of yours and tied the bells to your fleece jacket. Now just like a little pet, we can always hear you coming and going. I swear, Jack, don't make me get the leash!

I'm sitting in Peet's Coffee sipping an iced tea. I looked over the gorgeous full-color backyard plan that Gregory brought over today. As I write this, very envious busybodies are passing my table with their overpriced yuppie coffee, peeking at my garden design. Maybe they think I drew it and that I am a brilliant and talented landscape architect. Why, I think I'll just slide my glass of tea right over Gregory's name here at the top. There, much better. Now I'll sit here and admire my work.

In only three weeks' time our ugly suburban backyard will have symmetry, contrast, structure and continuity. We will have brick decks and a reseeded smaller lawn and a foot path leading to the bench near the cherry tree. There will be border plants of Spanish lavender, Korean boxwood, New Zealand flax and silk tassel. Last night I excitedly showed Papa the garden plan. He was still tired from sodding the front yard. He said, "That's nice, Babe."

He is *so fired* off my future psychic-gardening cable show.

Chop-Chop, you were so well behaved this weekend. We just returned from Ron and Naomi's wedding reception which was at Charlie and Tracey's house in Santa Cruz. We had a great reunion of our extended family. Aunt Carol flew up from San Diego and Pucci, Mr. Louie, Barbara and Wendy drove down from the city. Everyone thought you were so good natured. I tried to explain to them that it just seemed easy because there were ten people to take turns watching you. Usually it's just Papa and me. That's when the inmate truly runs the asylum.

Saturday we spent most of the day lounging around Charlie and Tracey's house. We spent way too much time in the morning watching Ron on his computer at www.swell.com or www.surfline.com so he could catch the surf cam of the day. I shook my head in disbelief at how seriously the lengthy surf drivel was being taken. After an hour of beach analysis between Ron and Charlie, the decision was made not to surf at all because the waves were not right and the tide didn't fit into the hectic schedule of our busy weekend. Thank God that was over. It was painful to watch. Like one of those bad movie shoots I've been on where no one can make a decision.

Oh wait, that's every film shoot!

We brunched in Charlie's prolific backyard on champagne, smoked salmon, sage-and-egg-white frittata and endive, arugula and tangerine salad. Charlie dressed Ron up in a clean, white linen shirt and handed him a tray of golden papaya and crab salad. Then he shoved him out the kitchen door and directed him to serve his guests. Charlie believes every straight man needs a gay coach. I'm starting to agree with his theory. Ron has the king-sized collector's edition of *Surfer* magazine on his bed stand and 240 unread e-mails on his computer. What kind of person is this?

He definitely needs a gay coach.

In the evening we went out to an elegant dinner where everyone took turns taking you out to the balcony so you could stay in motion. Your favorite partner of the night was Barbara. The two of you spent a long time outside looking for the moon. "Mama, the moon is behind the clouds," you love to explain to me on cloudy nights. I watched you with Barbara. She was holding you so warmly in her arms as you explained your celestial theory to her, pointing to the sky.

We spent most of Sunday morning playing on the beach. By early afternoon we had to pack up and get Aunt Carol to the airport and head back home ourselves. You cried hysterically all the way to the airport. Poor Aunt Carol sat next to you in the backseat. I could just imagine what was going through her head, thinking of her impending motherhood. I'm sure she's praying her child won't cry so loud and so long. I'm sure she thinks I'm the worst mother because I can't control everything you do. That's what I used to think before I had a child. *Why can't those mothers do something!!*

Once we dropped Aunt Carol off at the airport (she pretty much jumped from the moving vehicle), I missed her instantly and was sad. You were still pretty upset, so I joined you in the backseat. I took you out of your car seat, wrapped you in your fleece blanket and held you on my lap. We cuddled together till you fell asleep. I was thinking about Ron and Naomi. This is Ron's second marriage. His first was to Deborah, another great woman but much more outspoken than Naomi. Naomi is from Japan and barely speaks English, although she is learning quite fast. I asked your papa if he thought it was strange to marry someone you couldn't easily communicate with. "Is that what all men want?"

No answer.

"Bill, are you listening? Did you hear what I said? Do you think they argue less? How can they argue? How can they know what they're arguing about? Do you think their marriage will last longer than the rest of ours? Maybe a language barrier is a good thing?"

"That's nice, Babe."

"Bill, is that what you want?"

"Babe, you were right and I was wrong."

Sigh.

Barbara and Wendy taught him that line this morning over breakfast. Just say, "You were right and I was wrong." They told him it was the key line to being the perfect partner. They forgot to tell him to put some sincerity into the delivery.

Today we bought fava beans, red clover seeds and fetch. This afternoon you and I will plant these cover crops in the vegetable boxes to nourish the soil for next spring. We'll toss the old peppers and tomatoes into the compost pile and turn the soil in the boxes. We'll take the plastic off the one box we solarized and pray we have a Verticillium wilt-free soil this spring. You are out here buzzing around, watering the giant sunflowers that every year, just as they bloom, turn their big yellow heads over our fence into Betty's backyard. Just another garden lesson I have learned: I may think I'm in control but I'm really not.

You look so happy and busy. You always seem to be on a mission. And you never ever walk. Whenever you travel in your world, your gait is always something between a skip, a jog and a gallop. If I ever see you just walking, I assume you're not feeling well.

Later I took off some water drippers from the dripline of well-established drought-tolerant plants and plugged the holes with tiny pieces of black plastic called goof plugs (the most wonderful invention I've found at the hardware store). I was thoroughly enjoying the process. It was so satisfying to have a clear, well-defined problem and be able to fix it completely and instantly. Life would be so simple if we could just patch up all of our mistakes with an endless supply of goof plugs.

Sunflower

Botanical name: *Helianthus*
Family: Asteraceae
"Whaaa-whaa" rating: 3

Named after Helios, the Greek god of the sun, sunflowers actually come from America, not Greece. They were grown more for usefulness than for beauty. The oil is used for food, soap and paint, among other things. Sunflowers are tough, tolerant, mammoth plants that require full sun and lots of water. They are great seeds for children, or novice gardeners, to plant to feel a sense of accomplishment.

SEPTEMBER

"You Are My Sunshine"

Dear Jack,

The backyard is starting to lose its weeds-and-dried-out-lawn look. Some of the steppingstones are set in the ground, and a few of the new plants have been set along the border (strawflower, sagebrush, English lavender, hop bush and silk tassel). We installed a timer in the garage that automatically turns on the drip system. Seven zones go on automatically. I don't even have to press a button. I dragged Betty over and made her watch each zone go on. We both just stood there in amazement.

Yup, that's as thrilling as it gets around here. . . .

Later on, you and I went shopping for new shoes, built wooden towers and went swimming at the community pool. We spent the evening outside on the deck with the little Christmas lights turned on eating strawberries and talking about the moon. All around us was the disheveled yard with tools, lumber, cement, plant containers, bricks, stones and pieces of drip system strewn around. We hardly noticed it. To you, this mess probably looks normal—like your room. You were very busy holding your torn little bunny in your lap and watching all the airplanes pass by on a busy Friday night. With each one that flew over, you'd excitedly jump up, pointing to the sky, and say, "Mama! There's Grandpa's airplane flying to the moon."

❧ ❧

It's been a difficult week. Papa and I have been getting on each other's nerves a lot lately. We're both tired and never seem to have enough time alone together or by ourselves. We're so busy all the time. Busy with life and busy being "your people." And now we're getting cranky. I noticed it a long time before Papa did, because women just have an innate sense for suspicious emotional activity in both men and women.

Last night we tried to talk but kept arguing and getting nowhere. I couldn't sleep. I watched him sleep. He tossed and turned constantly like he was trying to shake me off. When he left for work in the morning, I wandered around the garden trying to figure out marriage. Is something wrong with us? Is it normal to describe your marriage as *Spy vs. Spy?* Always working undercover in covert psychological operations, we are masters of strategy, scheming more time for *me,* and how can we sucker-punch the other one into thinking we are doing what's best for all? We have turned into fantastic scorekeepers.

What happened to really wanting the best for each other?

Before I made myself any gloomier, the phone interrupted. I could hear Grandpa leaving a message on the answering machine. "Annie, I moved some money out of your mutual fund. The market is looking lousy. Let's just sit tight." I ran inside and grabbed the phone. I couldn't have cared less about investments. I just wanted to hear his comforting voice. We talked for a few minutes about you. I tried to sound like everything was fine, but as I said good-bye my voice quivered just enough that only a loving parent would notice and he said, "Annie, what's wrong? You don't sound right?" I cried to him about how unrealistic marriage is and how overrated it all is. "Why is everyone in such a big rush to get married and have *babies*? And why does everyone else make parenthood look so easy and so . . . enjoyable? It's no picnic. It's so much work and responsibility and monotony. And so long term. It worked centuries ago because people lived till forty, not ninety! Something is just not right about such a lengthy commitment. It's a system set up to fail."

No response.

"Dad? Are you still there?"

He gently, and in a very concerned and fatherly tone, said, "Look Annie. You're just tired and overworked, and so is Bill. It will get easier. The only way to work at marriage is by taking teeny tiny steps. Don't expect miracles. Don't be drastic right now. Just take *teeny-tiny* steps."

It's midnight. I have to be up at 5:00 A.M. for an absolutely ridiculous commercial shoot. We're already shooting ads for Christmas items— in September. This should push me right over the edge. I can see it now. I'll be stalking the Craft Service guy for chocolate all day while fighting with Huey about WOOF and how I don't think it's funny anymore while surrounded by a set decorated in mini-Santas.

But I'm taking *teeny-tiny* steps. I set the tea maker for 7:00 A.M. so Papa could wake up to a warm cup of green tea. I noticed he put my travel cup on the kitchen counter with a stick-em note, "I'll miss you. . . . " Now I know he's taking *teeny-tiny* steps too, as I suspect he'll miss me like a big fat hole in the head.

Are we really just miserable people living our miserable lives miserably? I decided my confusion regarding marriage demanded input from those I consider experts on the topic. I consulted my six-and-a-half best girlfriends. After quizzing them each on what makes their primary relationship work, they came up with useless, ineffectual and empty advice, and generously showered it on me:

"Send Bill to a mountaintop and run away to Paris."

"Stop eating so healthy; that's why you're miserable; it's boring!"

"Whiskey one night and Sake Bombers the next."

"Have more babies!"

"Wrap yourself nude in cellophane."

"Watch SNL reruns religiously at noon each day."

"Just get stoned a lot."

Where did I find these people?

Elissa's suggestion was the only constructive one of the bunch; each partner is to write a list of things that make them happy. I quickly and effortlessly wrote a list of twenty things that would make me happy. Papa wanted to wait and write his list during halftime of a Cowboy-49ers football game. He wrote his marriage vows during a Giants-Dodgers baseball game. I'm certain he'll be writing my obituary during a Redwings-Avalanche hockey game.

One of the first things I wrote on my list was to stop apologizing. Women are always apologizing for everything, every feeling we have that isn't all sweet and nice. Well, guess what? I'm *not* sorry. And here's another news flash: Women think about sex each day just as many times as men do and, by the way, in much more creative ways.

Note: Above sex statistics arrived at from a national poll taken of me and my six-and-a-half best girlfriends. Are we healthy, sensual, assertive women comfortable with our sexuality, full of passion and joy or . . . sluts?

Too close to call.

❧ ❦

Today we are at Goose Lake in the northern Sierra Mountains on a camping, rafting and cycling weekend. You are at your cousin Ryan's house. We decided—well, actually I decided—we would read each other's "happy list" out on the lake. There we'd be relaxed and not too defensive. Our only escape from facing each other eye to eye would be to jump into the icy cold lake. I could see Papa's agitation. He wasn't really too thrilled about being out on a lake trapped in a raft while I read off my marriage wish list. Once he paddled us out to the middle of the lake, I proudly pulled out our lists. And then the most amazing thing happened: In the blink of an eye, large ominous charcoal-gray clouds filled the sky and a thunder and lightning storm enveloped the lake. We began paddling frantically, with Papa laughing uproariously all the way to shore. He was convinced it was no less than divine intervention . . . or maybe just Menz.

We are back inside our cozy tent. Papa is reading *ESPN* magazine while I read *Raising Cain: Protecting the Emotional Life of Boys*, by Harvard professor and child psychologist Daniel J. Kindlon. He writes: "Maybe the biggest place where the catalyst for change will come is from the father/son relationship. If fathers serve as a model for a more emotionally literate manhood, sons will follow suit." Well put! Why does the *processing* of emotions seem like I am speaking Klingon to most men I know? Could they just go after the Pod People and get back their emotions?

After all these years, I'm still trying to crack the code on men. Tough crowd.

Sometimes on the set, when there is time for a quick personal conversation, I earnestly ask the predominantly male crew questions about their marriages. I constantly hear the guys say, "Why should we fix something that isn't broken?"

I know. I probably shouldn't be discussing "relationships" with the grips.

One day the entire grip crew showed me their chin scars, most the result of stitches they'd received on one of their many trips to the emergency room during their wild boyhoods. According to the grip department, a boy's thought process goes like this: attraction, action . . . thought! Then by age nine the thought part becomes irrelevant and is discarded.

Then they grow into men.

Wow. We are more screwed than I ever imagined.

The rain is making a perfect pitter-patter sound on the roof of the tent. It reminds me of your little feet speeding across the hardwood floors as you race to greet me each morning. Sometimes you're in a good mood and sometimes in a sassy or very, very frightening mood that makes us want to run for our lives. We never know what mood you'll wake up in, but simply seeing your face each morning makes us feel very lucky.

So Papa and I are taking teeny-tiny steps toward being nice to each other. It's actually working. The only time he got on my nerves was when he was waving his arms as I intentionally tried to run him over because he was acting as if he'd written the book on "backing up a vehicle in the wilderness."

You missed a spectacular storm last night. We were eating dinner on the patio of the Buckhorn restaurant in Sierra City. We hadn't been seated five minutes when a colossal black cloud filled the sky, and rain began pouring on us. All the tipsy tourists began scurrying around with their overflowing wineglasses and soppy plates of corn on the cob and barbecued ribs.

In the middle of the excitement we ran into Karen and Pierre, some neighbors of ours from back home. Karen and I stood under the doorway canopy with some of the other diehards and watched the thunder and lightning storm. Karen has a grandson who is about to turn two. We talked about how you would be fascinated by the storm. I told her if you were here, you'd be bossing me around saying, "Mama, more thunder, more lightning," as if I were in control. Then you'd have a tantrum if I told you there was nothing I could do. She told me sometimes the "terrible-twos" continue through the "terrible-threes." Then she said, "Go have another drink!"

Papa and I finally got a warm, cozy table near the fireplace and finished our dinner. We topped off the meal with peach cobbler and homemade vanilla ice cream. Amazingly enough, our tent survived the storm. The inside had remained bone dry. We tucked into our sleeping bags and read magazines by flashlight. I found a local magazine with an advertisement for the "Original Crystal Bluebird of Happiness" that sings *Zip-a-dee-doo-dah* as it spins in circles on top of your desk, only $16.95. A little lightbulb went off in my head: Mr. Louie. I filled out the order form and, feeling really good about myself, whistled *Zip-a-dee-doo-dah* there inside our tent. On the other side of the thin nylon wall, the storm raged through the black mountain night. Papa fell asleep first. I kissed his face.

My last thought before falling asleep was of the Queen Bee. I didn't tell her that we were camping because it makes her worry. I can just hear her: "Uch, sleeping in a tent in the middle of nowhere in the rain? What's with them? Meshugah! Why does she do this to me? Is this how I raised you? If you're going to be stupid, don't tell me. Just call me when you get home."

The scary thing is, I have a feeling I'll be speaking those same words to you one day.

We woke up to a spectacular morning. The storm clouds had moved out and blue skies were all around us. We had tea and cereal at the campsite table while we read each other our "happy list." We stayed focused for two hours—most of the time we were constructive and solution-oriented. The hard part is trying to make the solutions work in everyday life. We agreed that the combination of marriage and parenting is quite tricky, and trying to get the balance just right is extremely difficult. We also agreed to stop blaming each other and try with all our might to communicate clearly with one another without being afraid to speak our true feelings, to not become defensive, to really listen, to be partners not enemies, to admit our own faults (imagine that!) and to strive to be courageous role models for the next generation by acting like mature, healthy, conscious adults (imagine *that!*).

So, let's recap: Depending on what day it is . . . marriage can heal you by wrapping you in its safe sunny blanket of unconditional love, or it can stomp, pulverize and blow your feelings into tiny powdery emotional bits.

❧ ❧

After breakfast we drove to Goose Lake for a long, quiet rafting trip. The lake sparkled in the sun like crystal. It was early in the morning and we were the only ones out on the lake. It was so peaceful. I rowed for a long time, trying to strengthen my arms. Each time I turned the raft in another direction, I could tell Papa was just dying to critique or "help" me, as he says, but he couldn't. His being less critical was one of the things on my "happy" list. Although he's very well intentioned, sometimes it's just fine to let me do things my way, even if it's the wrong way. I don't know what it is, but there's something so exasperating about having him correct me. It chips away at the little bit of self-esteem I've managed to hold onto. I could tell he was busting up inside, dying to correct my imperfect rowing technique, but I just kept rowing and whistling, "Zip-a-dee-doo-dah-zip-a-dee-day."

Papa and I just completed a two-hour bike ride through cutie-pie mountain towns and then found incredible fire roads surrounded by wildflowers where we biked up to the highest peak. On the way back to the tent there were hardly any cars on the road, just the two of us silently cycling past the lumber yard, cattle ranches, tree-lined streets and beautiful old barns reminiscent of those found in your *Old McDonald* storybook. I rode back tired but feeling really happy that our marriage was getting back on track. Although I'm not sure if I should credit the long talks we had or my new religion . . . mountain biking. A warm breeze blew by and low-lying cotton-candy clouds drifted lazily above us as our ride ended. They were so close you'd think you could just step up onto them and take a teeny-tiny nap.

It made me think of you.

We have been busy traveling. The three of us are in Twin Falls, Idaho, for a few days visiting Papa's oldest sister, Debbie. The minute we arrived at her beautiful home, you found the toy lawn mower in the garden, belonging to Debbie's grandkids, and you've been mowing like crazy; the lawn, the living room carpet, the kitchen floor and the dog's coat. With you loudly and meticulously mowing around us, Debbie and I discussed her latest work venture. Each morning you can find her studying the obituary section of the local newspaper. Sitting next to her ceramic kiln surrounded by newly formed pottery, she hunts down dead people to make them their final sale. Tomorrow she goes to the local mortuaries with her truck full of urns. Within five minutes of our arrival, she began earnestly suggesting that we reserve an original urn for each other.

I'm getting the feeling this could be one strange week.

"You just can't turn off motherhood." Well, Jack, that just about says it all. That's what Debbie said this morning as tears dripped down into her scrambled eggs with salsa. She was commiserating about her four grown kids who keep her worrying around the clock. You just can't just turn off motherhood, my point exactly. Isn't she brilliant?

We couldn't come up with any great solutions for her kids' and their friends' full-body tattoos, body piercings, drugs, strip bars, unemployment, teenage smoking or deadbeat dads, so we hit the road. We kissed Debbie good-bye and headed to the Sawtooth Mountains of southern Idaho, singing "Skinnamarink-a-dinky-dink," thankful that we had an adorable two-year-old in the back-seat and not a tattooed and miserable seventeen-year-old, demanding to listen to Limp Bizkit or die.

We stopped in the town of Hailey and had a picnic on a small piece of lawn off the main road. There were several wild holly-hocks standing six feet tall along the side of an abandoned gas station. You and I collected a bunch of seeds to bring home. I tried to hide the resentment and jealousy I was feeling at perfect hollyhocks practically growing out of the pavement. While I sat on the grass with Papa and greedily counted my seedpods, you ran circles around us like a rabid dog on speed, wearing your brand-new purple plastic Jackie O. sunglasses.

In the next town, Papa and I found a field right near the train station to play Frisbee. You were so enthralled with the old trains and the nice passengers waiting that you even sat still for a short while. . . . Imagine that. For years I have been telling Papa what a great Frisbee player I used to be back in high school. My sisters and I would go to Central Park every day after school and play long, intense Frisbee games with the parkies. We'd meet at the bandshell or in front of the Metropolitan Museum and toss the Frisbees through the water fountains, just barely missing some poor tourist's head. It takes me about twenty minutes of warmup till I get my old long and fluid throw back. This is difficult for Papa to endure because every single one of his Frisbee tosses is absolutely perfect. He played ultimate Frisbee for years and he's a big showoff. Okay, maybe he's not a showoff. He is *so* not a showoff. He is such a good person and not showy.

So there we were. He throws beautiful, fluid straight throws each and every time, and I'd return a lopsided throw in every possible direction, except anywhere near where he was standing. This went on for a good while and just when he was getting all pouty, wanting to hang up the whole idea of us playing ever again and really questioning that I ever knew how to actually throw a Frisbee straight, I got back my old throw! For me, it's all about letting go. And we know how hard it is for me to let go of anything. Why should Frisbee be any different? If I wait too long, it's a screw up and I will hate myself. But if I let go at the very right second, it flies and flies and flies across the field right up to Papa's astonished and proud face. I try to be cool and contain myself, but inside I am dancing around the field, jumping up and down, feeling that I am so freaking amazing! Each time I do a good throw, you run over and we do high fives and climb up on the big rock next to me and we dance around chanting, "Sweet Sassafras! I am the bomb!" And I am so in love with my Frisbee partner and I am so proud of myself for hanging in there. It's all about letting go.

I think. Or is it about competition? Is it just *Spy vs. Spy?*

Too close to call.

Later we arrived in the town of Stanley. The mountains surround us in all directions. It's a rustic paradise here. Outside the fall weather is breathtakingly beautiful. There are a few perfectly placed puffy cumulous clouds in an otherwise pure blue sky. We're sitting out on the deck of our motel, which looks out over the Salmon River.

We spent part of the day with Papa's niece, Krista. She is Debbie's seventeen-year-old daughter, a beautiful and smart girl. She's spending the summer working at a ranch here in Stanley. This morning the four of us went for a canoe ride on Redfish Lake. You sat on Krista's lap and sang "You Are My Sunshine" the entire way out. On the way back Krista and I discussed the movie *The Wizard of Oz*. She claims you have to listen to the soundtrack of Pink Floyd's *Dark Side of the Moon* while watching the *Wizard of Oz*, though she never said exactly why. She looked surprised that I didn't know that. *Does everyone know that?* Or is it just a teenage cult thing? I think I lost some points with her on that one. She used to think we were hip and cool, and now she probably thinks we're dull and mundane like all the other parents out there.

So here we are—just you and me sitting on the dusty front

porch of our motel. Papa and Krista went for an afternoon hike. Across from our motel is the town store and the old 66 gas station. You and I are counting the few trucks that pass us here on this quiet country road. You found an old broom behind the motel door and are sweeping the gravel driveway. Good luck. You haven't realized yet that you're not getting anywhere, but whatever keeps you busy is just fine with me.

It's so quiet out here. Whenever a truck goes by we get all excited and you begin to tell me a story about the truck driver, then halfway through your sentence, you can't think of the right word so you just stare at me for a moment. I can almost hear the wheels spinning in that brain and then you just go back to sweeping.

We have nowhere to be. No phone. I have nothing I must do. I simply watch you. I feel as if time has finally stood still.

We have been home from our vacation for only two days and already we are back in the fast lane. I long for our little riverside motel in Stanley, where the last night of our trip, in the middle of a mountain rainstorm, Papa and I sat on the porch till midnight, drinking wine, laughing and debating what would happen if women ruled the world.

We had very different theories.

This morning I snuck out early to go for a walk up what I call PPD hill. This is where I walked with you in the mornings after many sleepless nights, as I tried to overcome postpartum depression almost two years ago. I was my own little Sylvia Plath carrying you around in the baby backpack and blasting the Allman Brothers "Stormy Monday" and "Whipping Post" on my headphones. I was afraid and absolutely certain back then that I would never adjust to motherhood. I spent a lot of the time looking like a deer in headlights, not sure which way to move. But we made it, Jack Dakota. We made it to the other side. Now I think back about those first few months when Papa and I paced our tiny house in circles at 3:00 A.M., holding you, as you'd cry yourself to sleep. Or when I'd have to jump out of a moving vehicle at the shopping mall while Papa circled around the parking lot, afraid that if we stopped the car, you'd start crying.

Now I can finally laugh about it.

On this morning's walk I thought about the time my friend, Barbara, came out from Colorado to visit. You were just a few weeks old. We were doing some errands and she was driving my car because I was too tired to drive. You were innocently sitting in your car seat in the back. As she approached a stop sign at a four-way intersection, I jumped out of my seat in a panic and begged her with tears rolling down my face, "No, don't *stop!* Keep driving. He'll start crying if you stop moving, and he won't stop. You cannot *stop!*"

She said, "Who will cry?"

I said, "The baby."

She asked, "You want me to run a four-way stop sign, at rush hour, so your baby won't cry?"

I couldn't take another second of my new so-called life. Tears started flowing. She looked at me as if she were thinking what a shame it was to lose a friend with so much potential, such a pity. Then she very gently and almost timidly, which is very unlike Barbara, suggested I find "help."

"I don't need help," I screamed. "I need a life! Please, Barbara, get me some work. I'll do anything: night shoots in the rain, maniacal directors, actors on drugs, primadonnas complaining that their motor homes aren't big enough, actors refusing to come out of their trailers, whatever. I'll do it. Just get me away from crying babies, breast pumps and happy new mothers! They're freaking me out! I'm not cut out for this motherhood stuff. Just toss me into the Stepford Wife Reject Pile and let me get some . . . *sleep!*"

We came to the stop sign and Barbara foolishly stopped the car. On cue, Mount Vesuvius erupted in the backseat. You howled and screamed the entire way home. Loud, angry, ear-wrenching shrieks. I'm sure, in your head, you were firing Barbara on the spot. She has a mind of her own. She won't cut it. She would never make it as one of "your people."

On the last part of my walk, I passed the bench where Grandpa likes to take you to sit and have coffee and a bagel. I thought about Grandpa. I remember calling him in those first few weeks and asking him how he was able to forgive me and my sisters for keeping him awake for years when the four of us were babies.

"Annie, you forget all that. You remember only the good things," he sagely replied. And he went on to tell me one of his favorite stories. He had just quit his job and had walked eighty Manhattan blocks, devastated and demoralized, trying to figure out how he'd support a family of six. When he opened the door to our apartment, Carol and I took our first few steps and did the drunken sailor walk, right into his arms. He often tells that story and I never tire of hearing it.

That same day I called the Queen Bee, wondering how she managed those early years with twin babies. I asked for her forgiveness. "I don't know how I did it either," she grumbled. "Uch, don't remind me. You really want to cry? You really want to suffer? Just have four teenagers. These are the good days, Mouse. This is nothing! Just wait!"

And, just in case I'd forgotten, she quickly reminded me that I was the crankiest of the four girl babies. "Uch, how you cried— from morning till night. How you took my kishkes out!"

I decided it was best not to call her again till my bout with PPD was over.

✼ ✿

You and I went for a long bike ride together today. Your bike seat is the only seat you don't mind being strapped into, so we do a lot of cycling together. I screamed "Yahoo" every time we went speeding down a hill, the wind blowing in our faces and you, in your bossy way, would yell, "No, Mama, *no!*" As if I wasn't allowed to have any fun! The more you yelled "No!" the more I yelled "Yahoo!"—just to mess with you. (Payback!) After an hour in the Petaluma hills, you started to get bored. We had a few steep miles to go to get back to the car and off you went, whining and wailing. I frantically raced the bike all the way back, uphill, and sang "You Are My Sunshine," over and over, out of breath, just to keep you happy. Each time I slowed down or stopped singing, your bossy little pipsqueak voice would order, "No, Mama, no. No slow down. More sunshine!" By the time we got back to the car, I was huffing and puffing and you sang in your merriest of voices, "You make me happy when skies are bwue."

We arrived home and called the Queen Bee for her birthday. She yelled at me for singing "Happy Birthday" all the way through. "Stop wasting my time!" Then you chimed in, wanting my attention. I couldn't decide which form of torture was worse at the moment—my mother or my child—so I took a long deep breath and tried to stay calm. Then I heard a click.

Five minutes later the phone rang. It was Aunt Carol yelling at me for hanging up on our mother on her birthday. Ten minutes later the Queen Bee herself called back, laughing and forgiving *me* for being rude! Before I could defend myself, you grabbed the phone and shrieked, "Happy Birthday Queen Bee!"

It was so good to hear her laugh on her birthday. I hung up the phone and sat pensively at the kitchen table. From the corner of my eye I saw Papa, eating an orange in the living room, shaking his head. He must've been wondering, again, how I am even remotely sane after so many years of dodging my mother's verbal bullets, riding her emotional roller coasters, and why I even continue having semipsychotic phone conversations with her. I hung up the phone and the three of us went out to the fig tree, as we do each year on Grandma Buba's birthday. The tree was a gift from her when we bought the house. We tasted the first few ripe figs, so sweet and "tasty," as you like to say. I was silent. Papa stared at the tree for a long time, looking very concerned, finally saying, "Babe . . . your mother is just weird."

Good morning, Jack Dakota. Happy Birthday to you! It is 8:31 in the morning. That's the time you were born two years ago. I was going to rush into your room at this historic moment and sing to you, but you just threw your cup of milk at Papa and he is giving you a harsh lecture and a long time-out. You woke up on the wrong side of the bed, I guess. It must be hard turning two, all that responsibility.

I was up early this morning planting fifty buttercups, twenty anemones, thirty gorgeous red tulips and sixty daffodils in the backyard. This time I put them in big clumps close together, like they do in Golden Gate Park at the Conservatory of Flowers. When they bloom in the spring, we can marvel how they were planted on your birthday.

Grandma Gin-Gin and Grandma Buba both called already to wish you a happy birthday. You were still in your extended time-out period because you would not say you were sorry to Papa, so you didn't have a chance to speak to either one. I told the Queen Bee how I thought of her this week a lot while the Master Gardeners were planting some fall annuals at the Redwoods Retirement home in Mill Valley. A couple of beautiful older women, each in their seventies, were wearing big straw sun hats and bright-pink lipstick while deadheading roses. They were gossiping about the few male residents who despite their many years, I was shocked to learn, still watched way too much football and otherwise didn't have much to say. However, the men were very much interested in a romance, preferably with a much younger woman and definitely with no strings attached. The Queen Bee chimed in, "What's so shocking? You think men are going to change? Mouse, don't hold your breath."

Then I told her how the women reminded me of her and her rose garden when she was a young girl in Israel. She stopped me midsentence and said, "What rose garden?"

"Ma, the rose garden your brothers destroyed."

"Those weren't roses. They were radishes."

"Radishes?! Ma! Those were *not* radishes."

"Yes, they were. I never had roses. My brothers pulled out the radishes and ate them."

My voice started quivering. I was getting really upset with this news. *Is this true or has she forgotten? Is she losing her mind?*

"Ma, don't go goofy on me! You told me they were roses! All different colors. I wrote a book about you and your roses. They have to be roses. I have a whole rose obsession based around your rose garden as a young girl. It makes me feel connected to you. It enriches my life."

"Uch, roses, radishes. What's the difference? What are you? A spy?"
Click.

We just put you to bed. You had a busy second birthday. Grandpa's message on the answering machine was definitely the highlight of your day. He had played "You Are My Sunshine" on the harmonica for you. You demanded that I play back the message eight times. Each time you concentrated intently on every note, as if you were critiquing his delivery, which I'm quite sure you were. At the end of the song Grandpa hit a high note to make a dramatic grand finale sort of sound and the message ended abruptly. Papa and I were both worried that he may have hyperventilated and passed out after his performance. We left him a message to call us back. No word from him yet.

After the harmonica performance there was a loud pounding on the front door. Only New York Mike knocks like that. I swear he thinks he's still back in Brooklyn. He brought you over a tricycle for your birthday! After giving you a big hug, he stood on the front porch ranting and raving about my garden. "Yo, what's all these trucks and sand and soil and pavers and people I've seen all week traipsing into your backyard. Missy Master Gardener?! She writes a book about gardening and then has her little peons doing all the work. What's up with that? Anyone can do that! Big deal. Shoot. Even I can do that. Get me some paper, a binder and a pen. I'm going to write a book about what a !@#$! fraud you are!"

"Mike, are you staying for cake?" I sighed.

"No, I can't be part of such a scandalous operation."

"Mike . . . you're a teamster . . . from New York. You live for scandal."

"Not today, baby. Today's Sunday—the Lord's day. I'm going to church."

"Oh, please."

Then off he limped toward the street, in his very type-A style, despite having had his third knee surgery only two days prior. His surgeon had told Mike at his age he should slow down, and Mike responded: "Get real. I'm !@#$! busy!" His mutt, Pepper, was patiently waiting in the backseat of the car all cuddled up in his child car seat. Off they drove to church.

Betty, Bec and our close friends Cat, Randy and Cosette came over with balloons and gifts. We had cake and ice cream and sang happy birthday to you. Bec sang her favorite song, "Skinnamarink-a-dinky-dink." Sweet Cosette gave you a bug box and some crumpled up, sticky, glittery paper that she referred to as "art."

Papa is now tucking you into bed and telling you a Blue Chip-Chips story. Blue Chip-Chips was a fictional character in stories that Papa's father used to tell him. You may think that your papa is a creative genius to come up with such an extraordinary adventure story each night. Well, let me tell you a little secret. He plagiarizes all his material from the Little Bear series you love so dearly. So next time I'm struggling trying to write and you see Papa rolling his eyes and explaining to me how overrated writing is, and that writer's block doesn't really exist and how any idiot can write a story, just ask him for some *original* material.

This evening, as the sun was setting, you and I were in the backyard. It was just the two of us. For a moment there was silence in the garden. You were in your own world collecting bugs to fix up your specialty, Rolley-Polley soup, and I was collecting hollyhock seeds. I watched you from across the yard, in amazement and bewilderment. I thought how lucky I am to have you in my life. I thought about how afraid of motherhood I had always been and how it was something I was sure I wasn't capable of, and here I am being your mother. I thought about the day you were born and how I held you in my arms, all cuddled up in your soft flannel blanket and itsy-bitsy hat, and how we gazed into each other's eyes. No spoken words. Just pure wonder.

Keep your heart open, Jack Dakota.

Plumbago

Botanical name: *Plumbago auriculata*
Family: Plumbaginaceae
"Whaaa-whaa" rating: 1

Plumbago auriculata (cape leadwort) is a must-have plant! This semievergreen sprawling bush does best in full sun, with little water once established. It is a fast grower and would do well on a fence or covering a wall. With support it can reach twelve feet. It blooms generous clusters of sweet, pale-blue flowers all summer long and into the fall. We have two of them, one in the front yard and one in the back. We barely pay any attention to either of them, yet they continue to grow stronger and flourish with more clusters of flowers each year.
Go get one!

QUEEN BEE JUNKIES

Tom Jones, Morphine or Bust

May 15

Dear Jack,

Well, that last entry was way too cheerful a note to end on. I'm back. I know it's been a while since I've written to you. I was taking a hiatus from trying to figure out the meaning of life and which day of the week "the end of the world" would fall on. I stopped planning what to pack and which lipstick to wear for the impending apocalypse. I was simply trying to enjoy life. But let's face it. It's just not me. I'm much more comfortable needlessly worrying about everything on a day-to-day, very exhausting basis.

Then I'm happy.

Two weeks ago I turned forty. I was slightly depressed about it. Actually, I was very depressed about it and I engaged in lengthy phone calls with my girlfriends Elissa, Cat and Ellen, commiserating about us all being forced to grow up. Bummer. One afternoon, with a bit of free time on my hands, I became preoccupied with what to do with these pesky gray hairs showing up on my head. I guess I needed bigger problems in my life.

And honey, they arrived full throttle.

That cataclysmic afternoon Carol called to tell me the Queen Bee had fallen and broken her hip. She, Uncle Scott and three-week-old

Baby Madison had taken Grandma Buba out to lunch. The diabetic Queen Bee celebrated her afternoon parole from the retirement home by drinking five cups of coffee and eating two pieces of cheesecake. As they were leaving the restaurant, Grandma Buba, buzzing on caffeine and sugar and feeling dizzy, was leaning heavily on Aunt Carol's arm. She suddenly tripped on the sidewalk and, as she was far too heavy for Carol to hold her up, fell to the ground screaming in pain. The paramedics quickly arrived and she was taken to the local hospital. The bad news was that she had broken her hip. The really bad news was that her kidneys had also failed and as soon as she recovered from the hip surgery, she would have to begin dialysis.

You, me and Papa flew down to San Diego for the weekend to see my mom and meet your sweet new cousin, Baby Madison. She is the *perfect* baby who sleeps all the time and doesn't make a peep. And to top it off, Aunt Carol looks happy! No sleep deprivation. No postpartum blues. Not one iota. I thought turning forty depressed me, but this threw me right over the edge. Because I was a tad bit jealous of Aunt Carol's calm and easygoing baby, I called anyone who would listen and joked about how my evil twin sister deliberately tripped her own mother on the sidewalk on Mother's Day and broke her hip. Aunt Carol overheard my phone call to Barbara and didn't think it was funny. I told her, "You don't think it's funny because you've got postpartum blues!" She didn't think that was funny either. She just flitted around her house doing her normal routine—humming, smiling, singing to the perfect baby and looking so proud of herself, so content and just plain happy with her new life.

What is up with that?

Nothing I said was affecting her, so I said, "You know what? You're not a real mother. This doesn't count. That's not a baby. She sleeps day and night. She doesn't even cry. That's a *doll*. You have no idea what real motherhood is. Sista, you are just one big *fake!* You are a *phoney!* That's exactly what you are." Baby Madison squinted her eyes at me from her tiny pink baby rocker and curled her top lip on one side. Her look spoke volumes: *"Lady, are you insane?"*

The following day, I spent in captivity, sitting with my mother in her hospital room. It was a few days after her hip surgery. There she was, the once fearless and fearsome Queen Bee, looking more pale and gray than ever before. I sat near her and read *Traveling Mercies* by Anne Lamott, a birthday gift from Papa. After all those years convinced he didn't listen, I realized he must be listening because he gave me a book written by one of my favorite authors. Just knowing that he heard me was in itself an incredible gift. Maybe I'm not so right about him after all.

That thought continued to haunt me as I watched over the Queen Bee. I started wondering what else I could possibly be wrong about. Oh, well, I quickly reasoned, it couldn't be too much. I mean, maybe, one or two things. Perhaps my front lawn project was a harebrained idea after all, and maybe I do place plants too close together and perhaps some of the songs on the Lilith Fair CD are a bit "male bashing." But just a teeny-tiny bit . . . and in a nice way.

Suddenly the silence was broken.

"Stop reading!" ordered the Queen Bee. I hesitated before I put my book down. Undaunted, I reached into my bag and took out my notebook and pen. I decided to take notes, stockpiling evidence and ammunition so when I returned home, I'd remember how stark-raving mad she made me, and how even from her

hospital bed, she carried on with her slash-and-burn method of parenting. Keeping notes would help me later to reason through my guilt for having kept my distance from her the past few years.

"*Stop writing!*" she demanded. I put away my notebook. I asked sweetly, "Ma . . . do you want to talk?"

"No. Just *go!*" she retorted dismissingly. It was just like old times.

Again I reached into my bag, taking out my Walkman. I put on a tape of so-called *calming* music. What a scam, I thought. They record the classical masters like Bach, Mozart and Beethoven, put a picture of an ocean on the cover, and sell it as "meditative and healing." I put on my headphones and tried to think loving thoughts. I remembered how important it was to my mother that each of her daughters had learned to play the piano and appreciate classical music. In between the incessant battles and skirmishes, she bestowed upon us so many gifts and so much love.

"*Stop moving!*" she shouted.

"Okay. We don't have to talk. I just want to be with you. I want to comfort you."

"Uch, see how she loves this? Now she's starting with me. Say it. Say how you love to watch me suffer."

Is she out of her mind? I wondered. *Or is it the drugs? Carol said the morphine helps with the pain and makes her nicer. Maybe she needs more morphine.*

"Ma, I hate to see you suffer."

"Don't tell me. Don't start with me. You're enjoying every minute."

What was I to do? Do I have it in me to turn the other cheek whenever she attacks me? I think not. Instead, I considered picking up the unused cafeteria straw resting on her lunch tray and blowing spitballs at her. But I didn't, for lingering childhood fears I'd get caught by Miss Hextor back at PS 6.

"What-a-bitch," the Queen Bee blurted.

"You're enjoying this," she continued. I got up and almost reached for the straw. I stood close to her face, speaking loudly and defiantly, "Guess what Ma? I am just now beginning to enjoy watching you in pain!"

(I didn't really mean it of course. I was just being . . . *bitchy*.)

Wouldn't you know it, the moment those vicious words came flying out of my mouth, in strolled Florence Nightingale, the goody-two-shoes nurse dressed in her spanking-clean white clogs, shiny white stockings and a pure white bow in her perfect blond hair. She had a saccharine smile and she called my scary mother "Sweetie." She looked at me aghast, as if she'd seen a . . . *bitch!*

After Florence Nightingale left, I sat there shell-shocked, watching my mother—not reading, not writing, not moving, barely breathing. I thought about the childhood bathroom where my sisters and I hid during her rampages. It was the only room in our apartment with a lock on the door. We never knew exactly when her "other side" would pay us a visit. It was always lurking, as unpredictable in appearance as it was in behavior. The erratic and wildly shifting mood swings, the never-ending displacement of blame upon others, the terrifying interrogations full of rage when she sensed we had seen our father, the hours of the silent treatment, followed by her self-pitying, "look-what-*they*-have-done-to-me" tantrums.

So, until we were old enough to move out, my sisters and I endured the best we could. We became trusted allies; we became survivors. In between homework assignments and babysitting jobs, we secretly strategized how best to tiptoe through the war zone we called home. Our pink, girly bathroom became our safe haven. Our secret weapon was Fluffy-the-golden-wonder-dog, who stood at the front lines, guarding and growling whenever she approached. We kept stacks of *Archie* comics, past issues of *Rolling Stone* and my all-time-favorite, *Mad* magazine, stored under the sink.

In times of uncertainty and fear, some find Jesus, some do drugs. I turned to Alfred E. Newman.

I stayed there till she fell asleep, only then, feeling it was safe to get up. I took the beautiful vase of my homegrown English roses and moved it next to her bed, so that when she awoke she'd have Ballerina, English Sachet and Abraham Darby right in front of her. Before leaving, I kissed her on the forehead and ran my fingers through her hair, like she did countless times to us when we were kids.

When I exited the main door of the hospital and felt the sunshine on my forty-year-old face, I ran and jumped for joy just to be out of there. I desperately needed a quick shot of Queen Bee anti-venom!

To my surprise there, waiting in the parking lot, was your grandpa. The Queen Bee had insulted him two hours earlier. When he couldn't stand it anymore, he left her room. In dealing with the Queen Bee you will never be heard, you will never be right and you will never win. The only sane, self-preserving and self-respecting choice is to *RUN!*

As we drove to Aunt Carol's house, I told Grandpa about my visit. I was drained and confused. He had just got off the phone with Aunt Carol. She had talked with Grandma Buba's doctor, who said that the Queen Bee had gone into renal failure. She'll have to begin dialysis three times a week for four hours a day. She was scheduled for surgery the next morning to put a shunt in her neck to allow blood to pass through. The two of us remained silent the rest of the drive home. When we got to Aunt Carol's house, Grandpa looked at me and said, "I don't know if I want to throw up or take a long nap."

I couldn't have said it better myself.

Note: To keep himself busy and useful, Papa has begun rating the Tommy K. art around the hospital.

Gooey and slightly misty-eyed: 1
Extra shmaltze with a backflip: 10
Florence Nightingale hospital wing: Tommy K. rating: 9.5

The next morning the hoity-toity vascular surgeon, Dr. Dilley-Dalley (that's just what I like to call him. I forget his real name), and his two little sidekicks entered the room. His posture was so full of arrogance that I could almost hear trumpets and see the red carpet rolling out for his entrance. *I can't say for sure, given his "medicalese," but I think he was speaking English.* He started with the shunts again and at that point the whole scene became surreal. I just didn't want to hear what he was saying. The shunts he had put in my mother's throat and arm were not working correctly, which had caused all sorts of complications for her dialysis, which is what she needs to stay alive. "Why, I've done thousands of these surgeries and I've never run into this problem." Dr. Dilley-Dalley spoke in a tone I believe he thought was reassuring.

I laughed deliriously and offered, "That's because she's the Queen Bee!"

He just stared at me. I didn't want my mother to be scared, and I was trying my best to keep things light and upbeat like she had done over the years whenever I had been afraid. But Dr. Dilley-Dalley had to be a party pooper! In as condescending a voice as he was able to muster, he spoke, "My dear, it's very frustrating for us and very discouraging for your mother, I'm sure."

Silence.

Trying to remain optimistic in the face of this dismal conversation, I chimed, "So what's the next step?"

One of his minions described in full medical jargon how they will try another shunt in her other arm tomorrow morning. At that Dr. Dilley-Dalley began to leave. I waved good-bye and tried to be peppy and positive. I said, "I'm sure the next one will work. This is the Queen Bee after all. See ya. Thanks for stopping by, guys. Thanks for a great day!" Grandma Buba smiled, waved just like Jackie O. and chirped, "Toodaloo."

The three of them stared at us.

Mother and daughter—lunatics in denial.

When I left that afternoon, I kissed my mom good-bye and said, "I love you, Mouse." She whispered it back and squeezed my hand. When I got back to Aunt Carol's house and told her about Dr. Dilley-Dalley and his entourage, she got mad at me for making fun of one of the top vascular surgeons. She said, "Ya know, Annie, at least surgeons deserve the money they make. This guy is trying to save our mother's life. He has a job that really matters. Not like those egotistical moron directors you work with making stupid TV commercials and violent trashy movies."

"Okay, sorry. I won't call him Dr. Dilley-Dalley anymore. And I'm really sorry I work with morons."

"Good."

"Do you think he was trying to tell me Ma's going to die?" I asked.

"No. I think you misunderstood him. I'll call him on my lunch break."

"Well, if he had spoken English it would've helped," I added.

"He was speaking English."

"Oh."

Well, what else could go wrong? Yesterday, while wrestling on the carpet with Papa, you fell and broke your collarbone. It was 7:15 in the morning and it was Papa's sister Aunt Cheryl's wedding day. We were at Grandma Gin-Gin's house. Papa had gotten up early with you to get ready for the wedding. I was just about to stretch out and take over the whole bed when I heard you scream downstairs.

An hour later we were in the emergency room, looking at a very nice X-ray of a crisply broken left collarbone. We didn't want to miss your aunt Cheryl's wedding day to her wonderful husband-to-be, Leo, so Papa and I took turns at the reception visiting with his relatives and holding you strapped up in a sling. You were so sad that you couldn't run around with your cousins Casey, Ryan, Gary, Stefan and Taylor. Grandma Gin-Gin carried you around a lot. You sat on her lap and she let you eat lots of cake and ice cream. Then you fell asleep for more than an hour in the car and I stayed with you and read the newspaper. Your papa's sisters—your aunts Tina, Cheryl, Denise and Debbie—came by with food and drinks to keep me company. Aunt Mammer-Jammer and her husband, Skeeter, came to visit every twenty minutes just to aggravate me. They insinuated that I was trying to get out of visiting with the in-laws and that I was hiding from another one of your papa's very loud and very long family functions!

Imagine that?!

If having a child with a broken collarbone and a mother lying in a hospital with a broken hip doesn't get you out of visiting your husband's relatives, I don't know what does. Tough crowd!

When we arrived home from the wedding, there was a message on the answering machine from Aunt Carol. Grandma Buba had just finished her third shunt surgery in her arm and looked horrible. I decided to call the producer of a two-week film project I was about to begin and arrange a replacement for myself. There was also a message from Aunt Augusta, who said she was flying to San Diego and would be at the hospital that evening. I was starting to get scared.

Augusta called early this morning in tears. She asked if I would fly down there as soon as possible. She said that our mom looked really bad. Knowing Augusta can be dramatic, and not trusting her analysis of the situation, I called Aunt Carol. When she sounds scared, it's time to worry, and she sounded petrified. Carol said Ma was not responding. Not eating or sitting up. I called Aunt Sha. We decided I'd fly to Los Angeles in the morning and we'd drive to San Diego together.

I said, "Sha, could this really be the end?"

All in one breath, and in her characteristic all-capital-letters speech, she spouted, *"I'll meet you outside baggage claim. Don't make me wait! It's a wrap!"*

❧ ❦

This morning I said a long good-bye to you and Papa. I felt so torn between my responsibilities to you and to my dying mother. I was a basket case. Yesterday I called Betty to come over because I couldn't move. I was stuck, sitting and looking out the window, immobile. She made me get up, move around and wash my face so I could look slightly sane when you woke up from your nap.

On the plane I stared out at the clouds and thought about my mother and how she hadn't eaten nor moved nor barely spoken for almost a month now. Someday her spirit will be up in these clouds, I romanticized as though adopting a child's perspective on death would somehow make it easier for me to accept the inevitable.

When I exited baggage claim and saw Aunt Sha's van waiting for me, I wanted to run into my big sister's arms and sob. Instead, as I opened the van door, she shouted, "She's sitting up, eating breakfast and chit-chatting with Augusta!" I stomped my feet, nearly dropped my iced coffee and screamed some very, very bad words, almost waking up Cousin Rebecca in the backseat.

"Carol tried to call you, but you had already left for the airport."

"!@#$!" More bad, bad words.

Your cousin Rebecca slept while Aunt Sha and I rehashed our childhood for the entire two-hour ride to San Diego. There was so much good and so much bad. Aunt Sha wasn't buying the nice memories. She was having trouble remembering those. I was tired and she was angry. We sipped our iced coffees and spent a long portion of the drive discussing new and improved methods of "throwing Mama from the train." Aunt Sha had had enough. I listened to her attentively. My thoughts went from one moment thinking how messed up she is that she doesn't want to deal with her sick and dying mother to the next moment thinking how incredibly healthy she is to have extracted herself from such an abusive and codependent relationship.

She's escaped! She's hopped over the fence, I thought.

I wonder what it's like on the outside.

And where am I in all this, Jack Dakota? Oh, just bouncing off the walls. One minute I'm still angry at my mother and the next I miss her madly and I want her approval on my new lipstick.

You figure it out. I've exhausted all possibilities.

We made it to the hospital and Ma was sitting up in bed. She looked very drained from her numerous shunt surgeries. One of her doctors came in and told us she would be transferred to a convalescent home tomorrow. He said she was doing just fine and walked out.

Just fine? This is what just fine looks like? I couldn't accept just fine when it meant seeing my mother looking so insipid and lifeless. I followed—well, sort of chased—him into the hall, past (yup, you guessed it) more Thomas Kinkade paintings hanging on the wall. (Enough with Tommy K! The shmaltze was so thick I could've tripped over it!)

I tapped the doctor on the shoulder.

"Excuse me, pal. Could someone around here stop to tell us what's really going to happen? Is she going to be okay? Should I take my Macy's commercial next week or replace myself?"

I could tell the Macy's thing just ticked him off. He stared at me in a peculiar way, surely thinking, "You self-centered Hollywood moron."

Just then my cell phone rang. I ignored it because his eyes were beginning to bulge.

"We don't know. She's made a miraculous recovery. We'll know in a week if she's going to improve or get worse."

Fine. I went back to the room to tell Aunt Sha that we won't know much for another week. Predictably, my update threw her right over the edge. She started packing up all her stuff. Aunt Augusta and I begged her to stay overnight and leave in the morning. We finally convinced her to stay after promising to baby-sit for Cousin Rebecca so Sha could get some rest.

Six games later of Rebecca's preposterous "I'm a little tea-pot" board game, I practically threw the poor kid and the tea pot into Aunt Augusta's arms. She took Rebecca to the hospital cafeteria. I was left alone with my mom. I usually cherished the times I spent alone with my mother. We always had very open and profound discussions about life, people, politics, books and films. Our talks never lasted long, though, and they just about always ended in a fight.

The Queen Bee was sleepy. I held her hand and she squeezed it often. Despite all the Queen Bee bashing I'd done on the ride down with Aunt Sha, my mother, once again cast her spell over me. I didn't even try to fight it. I fell right in. We were on cloud nine together. She whispered gently to me, "Annie, living is so hard and dying is hard too."

"Ma, what do you want to do?" I asked.

There was silence.

"Ma, whatever you want to do is fine. We're with you either way. We'll support you."

She shook her head in acknowledgment.

I felt guilty for not encouraging her to hang on. She refuses to do the physical therapy. She's in excruciating pain. She can't turn over, sit, stand or walk. She can't move. She can barely talk. Starting tomorrow, she'll travel in an ambulance from the convalescent home to the dialysis center three times a week while lying on a gurney the entire time. After four hours of filtering her blood through the shunts, she'll travel back by ambulance to her convalescent room. I just can't believe my mother will have to live like this.

I definitely need a Corona with lime and some Tums.

I put a pillow next to her arm and lay my head down. I quietly cried and sang her Tom Jones songs. One of my favorite childhood memories is cooking in the kitchen with her and listening to Tom Jones records together.

"She's a lady, whoa, whoa, whoa, she's a lady. She's a lady, whoa, whoa, whoa, she's a lady." Those were the only words I remembered. My mother didn't look too impressed. She just lay there resting, so I kept singing, getting louder and louder, testing her. *"Whoa, whoa, whoa, she's a lady, and the lady is mine."*

From out of nowhere, a chirpy Southern Evangelical voice chimed in, "Nina, I'm prayin' for ya!" It was the skinny, Bible-toting hospital minister that Aunt Carol had told me about. My mother would've burst an aneurysm if she knew he was poking his perky head into her room and "prayin' for her!" Does he get paid to be so chipper? Or is he so happy because he's doing God's work? Is he just a good person?

"Whoa, whoa, whoa. . . . She's a lady. . . ."

Today Grandma Buba sat up in bed and ate her entire pancake breakfast. She made small talk with Augusta and me as we doted over her, fluffing up her pillows, holding her cup and straw and giving her positive reinforcement. She even gave us a few small smiles. But the minute Aunt Carol arrived with beautiful Baby Madison, Aunt Augusta and I became chopped liver. Madison, the perfect baby who doesn't make a peep, stole the show. She lay down on Grandma Buba's stomach and fell asleep.

Aunt Augusta and I took a long lunch break while Aunt Carol stayed with the Queen Bee. We treated ourselves to lunch at a yuppie cafe and did some retail therapy to make us feel better. We were both nervous about the impending move to the nursing home. We didn't want our mother to be transferred. We liked the hospital. It was beginning to feel like home.

When we got back to the hospital, Grandma Buba was still very drowsy but a smile crossed her face when she saw us. Two cute young paramedics arrived with a gurney to take her to the convalescent home. Instantly, she perked up. They affectionately teased her and she flirted back! She ate up every minute of it. They asked her how many daughters she had, to which she lucidly responded, "Four." As they arranged to lift her onto the gurney, they asked her what her four daughters did for a living. She proudly told them. It was the first normal conversation I'd heard from her in weeks. Mario, the younger paramedic, began asking me questions about the film business. Of course, I gladly went on about myself. I explained to him how we film hospital scenes with extras dressed as paramedics and how we hire medical advisers to help us make it look genuine. I watched my mother's face as I spoke. She was listening and smiling proudly. I decided to keep going on about *me*, when Mario cut me off midsentence and said he was thinking about going to chiropractic school. I told him he'd have to talk to Aunt Carol, practically throwing him her business card.

Figures Carol would steal my show. She definitely is the evil twin! She is such a spotlight grabber!

I rode in the ambulance with Grandma Buba while Aunt

Augusta followed in our rental car. I tried to comfort her, talking sweetly, as I talk to you, Jack. I was telling her how strong she was and how she was going to recover and get out of this place fast. I begged her to do the physical therapy. She was quiet and for the first time in my entire life, she really looked scared.

Well, the party was definitely over when we arrived at the nursing home. I held the door open for the gurney as they wheeled her in through the backdoor entrance. I tried desperately to look brave, as I witnessed the apprehension and panic on my mother's face. I wanted to grab her and hold on tight, but I was trying to look strong for her. She was wheeled into a dark and sterile room. Her new roommate was a senile ninety-year-old woman who kept repeating like a parrot, "Hello? Anyone there? Hello?" I felt sorry for my mother but more sorry for her new roommate. The parrot lady had no idea what she was in for! Tomorrow they were going to start *forcing* the Queen Bee to do physical therapy three times a day. The thought made me laugh. Aunt Augusta and I smiled at each other. They have no idea who they're dealing with.

The nursing home depressed us so much that we decided to go get some decorations for Ma's room and get a late dinner, although we had no appetite. While the helium balloons we purchased were being blown up, we sat at the closed bank tellers station in a trendy supermarket. I sat up on the desk and Aunt Augusta sat in the bank manager's seat looking official but slightly dangerous. If anyone dared speak to us, they would've been skating on thin ice. They would've been very, very sorry. We ate packaged sushi, drank buttermilk from the carton, popped Alka Seltzer and tried to look remotely sane. Inside we were a mess—two emotional zombies lost in their own little world. Finally I chirped to Aunt Augusta, "Let's go have a drink! We need to get drunk!"

"You mean . . . alcohol?" She is only one step geekier than me.

"Yes, I mean alcohol. We deserve to drink."

"No thanks. I just want buttermilk. My stomach is upset."

"Augusta. Buttermilk? We need to drown our sorrows. Mask our pain. Let's get drunk! Isn't that what grown-ups do?"

"No, maybe some other time. And who said we're grown-ups?"

"Okay. I didn't really mean it anyway. It's just so *fun* to say, 'Let's get drunk!' Like we know how to drink and we are hip and cool, and we have options!"

Three buttermilks later, we returned to the nursing home with two-dozen flowers and twenty helium balloons. Aunt Carol and Baby Madison were there. We were so happy to see them. We needed support. Grandma Buba didn't notice the sunflowers and gladiolas or the big helium balloons. All she wanted was the perfect baby to hold.

At 10:00 P.M. we were about to leave when a nurse came into the room. She told us that a wheelchair would be here at 6:00 A.M. to take the Queen Bee in a van to the dialysis center. The three of us stared at her as if she were joking. Aunt Carol turned off her doting mother mode and turned on her direct and wise doctor personality. She went marching down the hallway toward the head nurse. Aunt Augusta went to get some water for the flowers. I proudly watched my twin sister and the head nurse down the hall.

"My mother cannot sit up. She can't move. She needs an *ambulance* and a *gurney* to go to dialysis. Not a wheelchair and a shuttle van. How could the hospital not inform you of that? Who is in charge here? I want to speak with them."

I turned my head for one moment and there, at the far end of the long hallway, was an old woman waving for me to come to her. I was deliriously tired but thought she needed help. When I reached her room, she snapped at me to help her get onto her bed.

I tucked her in but she kept yelling at me to put the pillow under her feet and not her head. I argued with her for a moment, but she kept telling me that I was doing it all wrong. Fed up, I ran out of there before I put the pillow over her face, which was looking more and more like the right place to put it.

Maybe Papa is right about another thing: I could never be a nurse.

When I returned to the Queen Bee's room, Carol yelled at me for leaving Madison alone with Grandma Buba. "What were you thinking? You can't leave her alone. Ma moved her arm and Madison fell off of her stomach and almost landed on the cement floor. Luckily I heard her and got here on time." I tried to explain to her about the stubborn old lady with the pillow but she wasn't listening. I felt terrible. I couldn't take anymore. I said I'd wait in the lobby.

Aunt Carol finalized the morning ambulance pickup and met me in the lobby. It was almost midnight. On the car ride home I was quiet and feeling very guilty about leaving Baby Madison alone. My tired mind kept visualizing all of the horrible things that could've happened. And there beside me was the perfect baby, sitting still in her sweet little pink car seat staring up at me, smiling.

This morning was the morning from hell. The ambulance didn't come at 6:00 A.M., though Saint Augusta sat there waiting with the Queen Bee. I arrived at 8:30 A.M., and the paramedics a few minutes after me. The Queen Bee looked pretty bad, but she smiled when she heard my voice. We traveled in the ambulance together while Augusta drove and met us at the dialysis center. My mother was surrounded by her paramedic entourage, while Augusta, me and two dialysis nurses wheeled her gurney through the front door.

There was a big commotion in the hallway. The medical staff

was discussing the fact that they could not do the dialysis with a patient in a gurney. She would have to sit up in a chair or they would have to send her to another facility an hour away. They were all very serious, forcing me to confront the gravity of my mother's situation. I wanted to pretend that if Augusta and I could just keep cracking jokes about all of this, it wouldn't feel so real or hurt so bad. But they went on and on about blood and tubes and shunts till I thought I'd faint. Ouchie! They were scaring me. Worse yet, they were discussing their bloody dilemma right over the gurney my mother lay on as though she wasn't even there. I snapped, "Excuse me, can you all move away from the gurney and find a solution somewhere else?" One of the nurses glared at me and instead of moving the horrifically detailed meeting about the impending torture to another location, she shoved me, Aunt Augusta and the gurney with my mother down the hallway and kept holding court among the nurses! I was so shocked. I'm used to barking orders on the set and crewmembers jumping! Wait till I tell Gwyneth, who also has major control issues, that I had absolutely no authority! She is going to howl with laughter.

I was just about to lose it when Jim, the head nurse, escorted me into his office. He sat me in a huge leather chair and said, "Tell me about your mother." The poor guy. What a silly thing to ask of me. Fifteen long and detailed minutes later, he got on the phone and instead of phoning me a therapist, he made a few in-house calls and worked out a solution to help my mother while I went to check on her and her entourage. He joined us shortly back in the hallway and said he would do dialysis on our mother only if we could get her sitting up in one of their special dialysis chairs. We asked Grandma Buba if she was willing to try. "No, no. Don't touch me. Don't move me. Annie, let's get out of here. Something's wrong with these people. They don't look right. Let's go. Now! *Quick!*"

It took eight of us to lift my stocky, temperamental and head-strong mother from the gurney to the dialysis chair. She screamed a little but it was a lot better than I thought it would be—at least she didn't curse anyone out.

With each problem solved, however, a new one arose. Anna, a kind Russian nurse, was having trouble connecting the tube to the shunt that Dr. Dilley-Dalley had repaired only a few days earlier. The dialysis folks were set to reject her again when our hero, Jim, stepped in and found a solution. All morning I rode an emotional roller coaster. Up and down, up and down. One moment I thought we were doomed and my mother was going to die. And the next there was a bit of hope and I kidded myself that she would live and be herself again one day.

Would someone please come collect me?

We sat with the Queen Bee for almost three hours. It was like her first day at camp. We didn't want to leave her alone till she made some friends. When we got back to the nursing home, Grandma Buba looked exhausted. Her roommate kept asking us, "Who's there? Anyone home? Hello?" Aunt Augusta and I looked at each other, feeling sorry for that poor woman. We predicted that if she didn't stop asking the same questions over and over, she'd be hearing from our mother relatively soon and it wouldn't be pretty.

I'm back home, sort of. I mean, I'm here physically but my mind is elsewhere and my heart is with my mother. It's a beautiful sunny day. I'm sitting in the garden near the princess flower that I pruned so severely last fall. I was worried that I had destroyed it, but it has come back and looks better than ever. It's close to six feet tall and the deep purple flowers are just beginning to open. This is a plant that is happy to please and so welcome at this dark and devastating time of my life. I can't seem to return calls or make plans. All I do all day is call the nursing home and Aunt Carol for any new developments. I'm not sure what I expect to happen, but I sure don't want to miss it. In the middle of most nights I wake up thinking about my mother. Last night I dreamed about the gold holiday boxes of fruit-shaped marzipan that she'd put under our pillows, with little love notes, when we were small.

John, my mother's cute physical therapist, begins to see the light. The Queen Bee likes him and tells him he's gorgeous, but she still won't budge. To her, physical therapy is out of the question. The screaming continues. The cursing accelerates. The nursing home family therapist meets with Carol and asks, "Does your mother have Tourette's syndrome?" Carol answers, "No. She's just . . . like this." The senile roommate requests another room "as far away as possible." The Queen Bee ends up getting the room to herself.

Next: World domination.

Grandma Buba is back in the hospital. After cursing out Nurse Anna, she had a grand mal seizure and developed another blood clot during dialysis. She was rushed by ambulance into the emergency room and is now in intensive care. Aunt Carol has been with her, holding her perfect baby in one hand and the Queen Bee's hand in the other. Carol sounds like she's finally hit her breaking point. We all left a few days ago and now there's this crisis. Fortunately, Grandpa flew in this morning to help.

Okay, that's that. Next shift. Grandpa has had enough. He was seen taking heavier than usual doses of his heart medication. The stress was starting to affect him. The few moments that Grandma Buba was lucid each day, she spent every bit of energy telling her ex-husband that he looked old. He left a few days ago. We are the reserves. You, me, Aunt Augusta and Deb, who arrived yesterday. We're refreshed, recharged and ready to jump back into the fire.

You brought her some lemons from Aunt Carol's lemon tree. (Yes, the tree still has many, many lemons. I swear I'm not bitter.) The Queen Bee was not herself. It was painful to watch her mental and physical deterioration. You played lemon toss with her. She smiled at you and called you "Da-ko-ta" in her sing-song endearing style that makes my heart melt. A minute later you slammed a lemon right into her broken hip. She yelled, "Get him out of here! What a wild animal! He should be on a leash!"

So we left.

We took a break. You and I spent the afternoon at our second home, the motel next to the nursing home. I bought you a turtle-shaped rubber float at the 7-Eleven and we swam around the small pool together for hours. It was the happiest I've been in weeks.

Later this afternoon you and I babysat for Madison while Aunt Carol went to the hospital and to work. She called me from her office. I told her that the Queen Bee had asked Aunt Augusta that if there is a God, where is he? Augusta had replied with one of her long, annoying, esoteric philosophical answers. "Uch," Ma said. "Uch, why does she answer a question with a question?!" Instead of laughing, Aunt Carol started crying. She had just gotten off the phone with the internist. He told her that Grandma Buba's abscess on her back was not improving and that both her feet would have to be bandaged because of bed sores. He said the situation was looking bleak.

Literally two minutes after I hung up the phone, I got one of those chipper, in-denial phone calls from Aunt Augusta that drive us absolutely insane. "Annie, Ma looks beautiful. She just ate. We're all fine." I hung up the phone and sat there in a daze. I just couldn't take it anymore. My brain was too tired and my heart was feeling numb. I had to decide: Either believe miracles can happen and my mother will get better, or start facing the reality that she is going to die. She can't walk. She can't sit. They lift her on a crane to put her into a wheelchair and a gurney in an ambulance to travel to dialysis. She's on thirty different hardcore medications daily. There's talk of amputating her foot. Her heart is bad. She has high blood pressure and is diabetic. She's not eating. She's in severe pain. She doesn't notice my roses anymore. And worst of all, she's beginning to not even notice when her grandchildren visit, the only thing that previously brought her joy. She is now merely a shell of the mother I once knew.

I sat on the couch staring off into space. Perfect Baby Madison was sleeping in her crib, while you, Jack Dakota, were tossing soggy moldy lemons into Uncle Scott and Aunt Carol's hot tub. I was numb and I didn't care, serves them right for having so many lemons.

This morning at the hospital the Queen Bee took a stand. During her second hour of dialysis, she ripped the tubes out of her arm and told the nurse she wanted to die. Two nurses rushed in to strap her down, medicate her and give her a blood transfusion. By the time Augusta and I arrived, the nurses were cleaning up the mess she had made and Grandma Buba was lying still in her bed, looking strung out on drugs.

While Aunt Augusta spoke to her, I sat next to her bed silently. I had absolutely no idea how to help. I needed someone to tell me what to do. Like . . . maybe my mother. She always seemed to know what to do and what to say. Even if she didn't know, she faked it amazingly well. She was always the ultimate optimist. "That's nothing! It'll pass, Mouse. Just forget about it. You'll see. Tomorrow will be better." And I always believed her.

And now I need her help. But she can't help me because she's too busy trying to decide if she wants to live or die. She's stuck somewhere in between, and as much as modern medicine is helping to keep her alive, it is also slowly destroying any dignity she has left. Maybe she's had enough. Grandma Gin-Gin told me the Queen Bee would die when her daughters let her go. I'm holding on so tight I don't know how to let go. If somehow I did let go, I'm afraid a part of me would die with her. I sit here beside her bed, not speaking a word, just holding her hand in mine, with my head resting on her shoulder.

Do we ever stop being someone's child?

Are we made to stand alone?

Yesterday we decided a meeting among the sisterhood was necessary. We had to figure out how best to help our mother. Aunt Sha drove down with Cousin Rebecca, and Carol took the day off work. Before they arrived at the hospital, Aunt Augusta and I stopped by the dialysis center to meet with Jim, the head dialysis nurse. He always gave us straight answers in a gentle way that didn't cause us to have a mental breakdown right there on the spot. He told us that with patients like our mother, there would always be complications. We were merely buying time by keeping the dialysis going. He showed us her chart over the past few weeks. Her vitals were going down slowly and steadily.

When we got back to the nursing home, Aunts Sha and Carol were waiting for us. We spent the afternoon together. For weeks we couldn't get all four of us to agree on stopping the dialysis, and we had been too afraid to ask the Queen Bee what she wanted. One of us always seemed to be willing to play the role of the dreamer, believing our remarkable mother was going to recover. Today's meeting got us nowhere. We felt we needed to ask our mother what she wanted to do before she deteriorated anymore. We voted for Aunt Augusta, the eldest, to be the brave one to ask.

Aunt Augusta went to the hospital early this morning. She somehow found the courage to ask Grandma Buba if she wanted to continue the dialysis. The Queen Bee wasted no time with her reply: "No."

Augusta reasoned with her: "Ma, if you stop the dialysis, you'll die."

"So, I'll die. Why is it your business?"

After discussing it with my mother's doctors and her rabbi, the four of us agreed to stop the dialysis. We spent the day watching Aunt Carol sign power of attorney papers and meet with hospice nurses. Our mother had always told us not to let her live in a condition like this. She had signed legal health documents years ago attesting it. We wanted to do what she wanted, not what anyone else needed.

I left for home this afternoon so I could spend the weekend with you and Papa. But when I got home, I was in no mood to be with anyone. Papa took you out to dinner while I stayed home and looked at old photo albums, searching for pictures of my mother and me together. I found one of my favorites. It's of me at twenty-two, sitting on her lap, hugging her. We're both posing and my legs are flailing in midair as if I'm about to fall off her chair. We're both cracking up laughing.

You and I flew back down today, carrying with me the last bunch of David Austin roses I will bring my mother. When I walked into her room, the aides were lifting her with the crane to put her in the wheelchair. I put my face right in front of hers and smiled. She said, "Hey," and a big smile enveloped her face. Her eyes lit up for a moment in a way they hadn't in weeks. She seemed so much happier without the stress of dialysis. Once she was set in the wheelchair, Aunt Augusta and I took her out into the garden.

Augusta then took you with her to do some errands while I sat in the garden, watching my mother sleep in her wheelchair. I stared at her. One moment she'd have such fear on her face, and the next she'd have the slight hint of a smile. I recalled my childhood spent trying to please her, my early adult life trying to understand her, and now I simply wanted to forgive her.

I closed my eyes for a moment when I felt a familiar tap on my shoulder. I turned around and it was my mother's beautifully manicured bright-pink fingernail tapping me. She was trying to reach for my hand. I moved my chair closer to her. Face-to-face, we sat merely inches apart from each other. She grabbed both of my hands in hers and kept squeezing my fingers and staring into my eyes, as if she wanted to say something. We both held on for dear life. I was waiting for her to speak but the words wouldn't come out. I took off my sunglasses, stared into her eyes and sobbed. I said, "Ma, I love you so much."

She just kept squeezing my hands. With tears pouring down my face, I said, "Ma, I'm writing about you and our life. You can have a whole chapter if you want." There was no reply. "Or you can have a whole book!" I added.

She nodded her head, yes. As if we were having a normal conversation, she shrugged her shoulders a bit, almost smiled and replied, "Of course." She then closed her eyes once more and I held her hands in mine until she fell back asleep.

While sitting with my mom this afternoon, I pulled out one of six books I had recently bought about death. I had gotten a little obsessed at Borders the other night. I don't know exactly what I expected to find in these books. I mean, dead is dead. Whatever I was looking for just wasn't there. I guess I was looking for someone to assure me that my mother wouldn't really be dead. Or maybe just a *wee* bit dead. I don't know why I bothered. I couldn't even get past the first few pages in any of the books. In fact, I hated them all. What a scam, writing about death. None of the authors have been dead. What do *they* know? I wonder if I can return them. . . .

Three downer books about death later, my eccentric aunt Fizz landed. One of my cousins, after one too many martinis, once described her as our family's version of the antichrist. She is my mother's little sister from Israel who now resides in New York City. She arrived in her usual combustible state—straight from the temple of the holy firecracker. She touched the ground running. Well, not quite running. She deplaned in a wheelchair pushed by some poor United Airlines schlep who had to listen to Aunt Fizz's litany of lawsuits and the story of her two broken toes before Aunt Sha could run over, seize her from the wheelchair and make her walk at a good clip to the car. "Everyone's so nice in California," she squealed in her half-Israeli/half-New York accent—a lethal combination. She enthusiastically hugged Aunt Sha and Uncle Jim, who were wearied and annoyed because she had missed her original flight and they had waited three hours for her at the airport.

Note: It's not good to keep Sha waiting.

Earlier this morning the sisterhood had called together a top-secret meeting, specifically on the subject of Aunt Fizz's arrival. She drives our mother absolutely berserk. Though they love each other, their relationship is one of constant crisis and combat. Plus, she is ultra-religious and my mother, God bless her, is suspicious of anyone too devout. We felt Fizz had the right to be with her sister, but we also wanted to protect our mother from Fizz's vexing presence. Because Grandma Buba had kept her distance from her family in Israel, we saw Fizz only every couple of years, like at weddings and at . . . okay, well, just at weddings. The four of us decided we would be patient and compassionate with Fizz at this difficult time.

Well, the nonjudgmental and compassionate idea lasted maybe five minutes, tops.

One short drive from the airport and Aunt Sha smelled trouble with a capital T that reverberated with a capital R, as in religious right. Fizz entered the Queen Bee's room and spoke in Hebrew to her semicomatose older sister. My mother stared and nodded her head as Fizz went on about their childhood in Israel. Fizz named all seven sisters and brothers and all the nieces and nephews. Grandma Buba seemed intrigued and alert. For a moment I thought this could be a good thing. But a moment later I realized I was just being naïve.

Fizz then handed me a book on Judaism and questioned me steadfastly about why I wasn't religious and why I was leaving in the morning. I tried to explain that I'd been in and out of San Diego for almost three months and that the four sisters were taking shifts and that I was taking a two-day break to make sure my life was still there. I told her I had to check in with my work and that I needed to see my husband and son. "You don't need to work," she declared curtly. "Let your husband work."

Not a good thing to say to an ardent card-carrying feminist.

Fizz next whisked out to the hallway and demanded the head nurse put our mother back on an IV and bring her some dinner. The nurse explained that at this point neither would help and they would only add to her sister's discomfort. So Fizz countered by threatening to sue the convalescent home. Aunt Augusta and I intervened in the hallway and begged Fizz to listen to reason. We were doing what our mother had requested of us, both verbally and written in legal documents. But Fizz wouldn't let it go and started a noisy scene at the nurse's desk. The patients hanging out in the lobby put down their newspapers and spun their wheelchairs around, descending upon us. I had flashbacks from a scene in *One Flew Over the Cuckoo's Nest*. It was quite a show. In the middle of the arguing and the negotiating between Fizz, Aunt Augusta and the head nurses, I worked the crowd, shaking hands, introducing myself as the Queen Bee's daughter, schmoozing and smiling to our audience. They seemed to be enjoying the show and I was glad we could supply some entertainment in this dreary, freaky place.

Dinner with Fizz, Aunt Sha and Uncle Jim was more of the same. Aunts Carol and Augusta had saved themselves from this pleasure by taking shifts with the Queen Bee. You'd think I'd be used to unreasonable people, having lived with my mother, growing up in New York and working in the movie industry, but Fizz takes the cake! She spent the entire dinner criticizing and judging us on issues she knew nothing about and telling us we shouldn't be leaving our mother tomorrow. We told her we'd be back in two days. We were all drained and needed rest and introspection so we would have the fortitude to continue. She just didn't get it.

I could tell Mount Saint Sha was about to blow.

Just as our Greek salads, Diet Cokes and french fries arrived, Sha erupted: *"Ya know, Fizz, our mother is lucky we're here at all. Any self-respecting person would not have put up with her and would've stopped contact with her years ago!"*

Fizz looked shocked that her sister hadn't been the perfect mother!

She said, "Your father hurt her by leaving and then you all left her. You hurt her so! You should all beg for forgiveness!"

"What?" I said. *What planet is she from? Planet Fizzy!*

We proceeded to tell her our version of childhood stories about our mother's mood swings and explosive temper, and how we found that the only way possible to love our mother was from far, far away.

Fizz said she was familiar with this violent behavior. She recounted how her father, Sava, would privately beat her and her sisters, while in public he would be loving and charming. She told us childhood stories about how Sava himself had been abandoned by his parents and left to live with his uncles, who mistreated him for years. And the stories went on and on—stories of abuse, stories of shame and stories of shell-shocked survivors.

I spoke up: "Fizz, here in the civilized world, we call it child abuse." She firmly disagreed and told me not to talk about it. "We have to talk about it! We have to confront the past, otherwise our children will absorb it. Perpetuating family dysfunction affects individuals and society as a whole. We have to stop the cycle of abuse. My sisters and I have made a pact to do whatever it takes to break the cycle. Are you with us, Fizz? You're burning daylight! You're either on the bus or off the bus." She replied, "Don't tell your husbands. They'll use it against you someday. You can't trust them."

She was definitely off the bus. In fact, she was not only off the bus, but the bus had left without her. I tried to reason with her, but it was futile. Fizz only heard what she wanted to hear. It was agonizing to be with her. I could see so much of my mother in her. They both had so much love trapped inside them, but they were conditioned at a young age to always be poised for battle.

Fizz didn't have a hotel room that night, so I offered her to stay with me at the roadside motel Aunt Augusta and I had called home for the past few months. Saint Augusta was spending the night in the Queen Bee's room at the nursing home. For some legal reasons I didn't quite understand, they wouldn't give her a bed, so she slept on the floor, at the foot of her mother's bed next to the Thomas Kinkade wall calendar.

That's our little saint.

Nursing home suite: Tommy K. rating: 6.2

Today you could call me a saint too—for not killing Fizz last night. Was I absolutely out of my mind to share my room with her? I'm so disappointed in myself. I thought this would be the perfect time to practice compassion. But there are some people who bring out the worst in you. I'd like to see the Dalai Lama maintain his patience with my aunt Fizz. I bet he'd be running for the knife drawer too.

I regressed into a mean and snippy teenager. I felt like I was arguing with my mother again. It was a very, very long night. It all began around midnight. First the talk was about Judaism, then about Israel, then about my poor dying mother and finally—the mother of all lectures—about why, twenty-five years ago, my sisters and I "didn't stop your father from leaving your mother?"

I said, "Hmm, Fizz, that's a timely and relevant question. Why don't you bring up the most painful time of my childhood while my mother lies on her deathbed?" I walked out and slammed the door, just as I did when I was sixteen. I went to a nearby pay phone and called Papa. It was late but he was awake (watching sports highlights, on videotape, so he could replay it as many times as necessary).

I said, "Hi, sports fan!" and then I cried for a long time on the phone. I told him about our excruciating dinner and how Fizz was stalking me in my motel room. I heard *Sports Update* end abruptly in the background. He actually turned it off. I felt so loved. But then I thought, Did he turn off sports to really be there for me or so that he wouldn't be missing any crucial highlight? He tried to cheer me up by telling me a story about Mr. Louie, who had just flown to Michigan to visit his hospitalized mother. Mr. Louie and Pucci would sit with his ailing mother for hours at a time, while her roommate, on the other side of the curtain, would pass gas every half hour for twenty seconds at a time. Mr. Louie, your godfather, would glance at his watch and time it: "Blzzzzzzzzzzzhhhhhhhh." I know it's juvenile, but we found it so funny we were howling.

When I arrived back at the room, Fizz was still awake! I quickly undressed, brushed my teeth and, when she turned the other way, jumped into bed and hid under the covers. She was rambling on about the Messiah coming and then about how much my mother loved her daughters yet we all moved so far away, leaving her all alone. We were sinners. Just as I was about to fall asleep, she decided it was the precise time to inform me that in the Jewish religion, by stopping the dialysis, we had sinned once again. She was insinuating that we were murdering our very own mother.

Hmmm, that's a comforting thought. I'll just doze off now and catch a few Zs.

Needless to say, I was up all night tossing and turning. Aunt Fizz called out my name hourly, trying to initiate conversation. But I hid under my blankets, faked a few snores and pretended I was asleep. I found myself thinking about ninth grade. Aunt Augusta was attending Hunter College then and driving a cab part-time to support herself. She had long blond hair and crystal blue eyes. She was the most beautiful NYC cab driver I had ever seen, and she possessed the gift of language to outmatch any big-mouthed truck driver in downtown traffic. Every Friday afternoon she'd pick the three of us up in her cab and we'd drive two hours, to the beach to play Frisbee. The four of us would sing along to Carol King; Crosby, Stills, Nash and Young; and the Eagles. With the windows wide open, without a care in the world, we had escaped. We were free.

I tried to continue having good thoughts, like how my mother had overcome a childhood of poverty, abuse and neglect. I saw her as an extraordinary woman and a courageous survivor. But each time Fizz made a peep, it triggered distressing memories and I'd see my mother as a fearless warrior on a psychological take-no-prisoners, search-and-destroy mission.

The next morning at breakfast with Sha, Uncle Jim and Aunt Fizz, I looked and felt like a derailed train wreck. There was nothing left inside of me. I sat at the table, eating my soggy Cheerios, staring into space. Aunt Sha saved me by doing all the talking. The discussion was about the funeral arrangements. Uncle Jim and Fizz discussed at length my least favorite and most skeptical topic of all: religion. Fizz, of course, felt that the reform rabbi, Rabbi Lenow—whom our mother had loved and respected because he was an open-minded and good man—wasn't as worthy as Fizz's scary, fanatical rabbi. She held in her hand what looked like a baseball card. On it was a picture of her rabbi and a phone number. It reminded me of the roadside billboard I once saw in Idaho with a huge semitacky painting of the Virgin Mary extolling motorists, "1-800-CALL-MARY." When religious figures are printed on baseball cards and have toll-free 800 numbers, this can't be a good sign.

The world is definitely coming to an end.

After breakfast we all went back to the nursing home. I lingered, not wanting to say good-bye to my mother. I sat holding her hand, staring at her, feeling so heartbroken. I'd be back over the weekend, but I didn't know if she would wait for me.

Aunt Augusta looked upset that I was leaving. Living in Alabama, it was difficult for her keep flying back and forth. She decided to stay. If staying wasn't difficult enough, staying with Fizz was absolute torture.

Aunt Carol took me to the airport. As we left the Queen Bee's room, Augusta was standing on one side of the bed with Fizz standing on the other, and they were arguing right over our semi-comatose mother.

"I'm not attacking you. Who's attacking you?" Fizz snipped.

"You've been attacking all of us since you got here," sparred Augusta.

"Now you're attacking me! I'm not attacking you."

"Yes, you are! You can't stop attacking me!"

"You stop attacking me, and I'll stop attacking you!"

"Me? Attacking you?!"

❦ ❦

This morning I woke up and questioned why I was at home when I should be with my dying mother. So I packed our suitcases and you and I left for the airport. You thought it was the coolest thing to wake up and spontaneously decide to be jet-setters. We took the bus to the airport. On the way we had hard-boiled eggs and orange juice. You sang "This Old Man" the entire one-hour bus ride. When it came to the line "Give a dog a bone," you'd sing, "Atta atta bone." I knew enough not to correct you because you'd get upset, so I just sat back and enjoyed the show.

Aunt Sha was just getting off the phone when we arrived at the nursing home. She had spoken to Bernadette, a bigwig with the San Diego Police Department. She was inquiring about how to get a restraining order, describing Fizz as "suspicious activity." I'm telling you, Jack, don't mess with your Aunt Sha. She had arrived yesterday to save Augusta, who was beginning to take on the appearance of a prisoner-of-war. As if it wasn't enough keeping vigil around the clock with our mother, we now had to schedule shifts of whose turn it was to be with Fizz. Her dialogue was constantly provoking and accusatory, and the minute she opened her mouth, one instantly felt the need to defend oneself.

Yesterday I got a call from Grandpa telling me not to give Fizz any information. "Just say 'I don't know' to everything." He warned us that Fizz has a history of filing harassment and disability lawsuits. It's been a bad joke in our family for years. Grandpa claimed he could smell "litigation!"

"Dad, you're in New York. How can you smell litigation?"

"Something stinks."

"What?"

"I'm telling you, Annie, she's cooking something up."

Aunt Carol stayed the lunch shift with Fizz and the perfect baby, while the rest of us went outside to get some air. Aunt Augusta fell apart in the parking lot, and the three of us had a huge argument. Augusta was tired and wanted to go home. She felt that for weeks she had carried the weight of the world on her shoulders, while the rest of us got to go home and take breaks. She was right, sort of. But Aunt Sha, in capital letters, was quick to remind her that she also didn't live close enough to go home, and that Augusta had taken time off from teaching and didn't have a stubborn and defiant two-year-old spitfire to keep occupied all day long at a nursing home. Aunt Sha wasn't about to let anyone make her feel guilty!

Oh, but I felt so guilty! Augusta and I had been together for more than two months, watching over our mother and protecting each other. Between Augusta and me, fighting was unusual. For weeks we had been each other's best ally, always finding the bright side of difficult situations and trying to make each other laugh. We had absolutely no plan and we were sticking to it! We'd sing annoying songs to the Queen Bee and endure unpalatable nursing home food while discussing philosophical theories, repressive institutions, why Viagra is covered on some insurance plans while birth control isn't and why the Equal Rights Amendment that was written in 1923 still hasn't passed through Congress. When the Queen Bee was still a bit lucid, she'd sometimes shake her head in agreement with us. I swear if she had had one more drop of energy she would've chimed in "Because it's a man's world."

But I did the best I could, Jack. I felt we all did our best. No one has the right to judge you when your mother is dying. You can never know how you will react or feel. Even the best planning leaves you pitifully unprepared. And if you have the courage to imagine your life ahead without your mother in it, you are left weak-kneed and empty hearted.

Today it's quiet in the Queen Bee's room. I'm here alone with her. Aunt Fizz has gone to the temple to pray for her sister. The hospice nurses are angels. They are our bright little lifeboats steadily sailing in with the morphine drip, oxygen and soft, reassuring words. They tell us that our mother is drifting on clouds. We tell them she may be drifting on clouds but we are certain she is still dictating the cloud movement—and quite vocally at that. Then there are the nurses' aides, who are all very young and energetic. They come in every hour to turn our mother. They speak to her gently: "C'mon, Nina, time to turn over. You can do it."

My mother used to scream in pain but now she just moans and lets them do all the work. There's no longer any attempt to hoist her into the wheelchair. She's looking pale and is now on oxygen. Her eyes follow me around the room, but there's a vacant, distant look in them. We play classical music around the clock for her. We wanted only for her to be at peace in her final hours, something she had difficulty attaining during all her years of living. I open the door wide to the garden so she can sense all the beauty surrounding her. Then I sit near her and hold her hand. Just when I'm having my moment with my mother, in barge all my loud sisters, two kinetic toddlers and the perfect baby.

We put cartoons on for you and Cousin Rebecca. Then I persuade my sisters to do a meditation. They must've been pretty emotionally desperate because they all agreed. Well, Aunt Sha we had to sort of drag over. The four of us stood around our mother's bed and closed our eyes. I asked everyone to think of our mother as a little girl, then to think of a happy time with our mother when we were little girls. It was quiet for a few minutes. I could sense Aunt Sha was rolling her eyes, so I kept mine tightly closed. Then we all rubbed our hands together and lay them on our mother's face, arms and legs. We sent her all the love we had, thanked her for believing in each of us, thanked her for all she had done for us, especially for all the years of brown paper bag lunches with little love notes, and we told her we were letting go. We promised we'd always be with her in spirit, just as she would forever be in each of us. A euphoric serenity enveloped the room like some kind of metaphysical harmonic convergence. When we opened our eyes, Aunt Sha ended our peaceful meditation by sighing "Uch," and loudly opening a can of Diet Coke.

I had the afternoon shift with my mother while Aunts Sha and Augusta kept you and Rebecca occupied at the park. Aunt Carol signed more legal documents for the Queen Bee. She went home for a break and gave me strict orders not to leave the room. Control freak! The control freak, Saint Augusta and Bossy Sha have been obsessed these past few weeks with having someone with our mother at all times. They don't want her to die alone.

It was 5:30 A.M. when the call we all feared broke the silence of our motel room. It was Aunt Augusta crying. "The sky is full of colors," was all she said. My stomach tightened; I knew immediately what she couldn't bring herself to say. Five minutes later Augusta arrived at our room. We quickly wrapped you in your fleece blanket, raced to the rental car downstairs, and drove like maniacs back to the nursing home. It was a beautiful sunrise, one I shall never forget. You rested in my arms as Aunt Augusta told us how the Queen Bee had taken her last breath. She described how the hospice nurse, Martha, had held one hand while Augusta had clenched our mother's other hand. Martha had said, "Nina, you can let go now. Go ahead. It's okay." But Augusta had countered, pleading, "Mommy, no, don't go."

When we arrived at the nursing home, Aunts Sha and Carol were already there. You gently and innocently kissed your grandmother on the cheek. Aunt Sha whisked you off to her hotel to watch cartoons with Uncle Jim and Cousin Rebecca. I pulled down the bed rails and moved my chair as close as possible to my mother's side.

I clenched her hand in mine, refusing to let her go. For what felt like only a few moments—which I later realized was three hours—I simply stared. It was dreamlike, almost hypnotic. My mother's face held a peacefulness I hadn't seen in her in years. The room too was filled with a profound stillness and was warmed by the rays of the early morning sun. In the background I could smell the sweet scent of jasmine as it drifted in from the garden. Despite a lifetime of hard work, her hands looked glamorous, accented by the peach-colored nail polish Saint Augusta had applied a few days earlier. Almost in defiance of her seventy-three years, her face had few wrinkles. She often told us that her secret was applying Vaseline around her eyes each night, and she frequently chastised us for wasting our money on expensive lotions. Lying there, she looked beautiful, like the English roses we both had loved.

Aunt Carol interrupted the quiet, talking of logistics, while Aunt Augusta packed up the Queen Bee's belongings. Aunt Sha returned and began planning "The Event." She's the only person I know who can organize an entire funeral in four hours, on a Sunday morning no less. Carol and I joked about the lines from a song, "Time Waits For No One" and reworded it: "Sha waits for no one."

I called Papa. He was on the next flight out of San Francisco. By now the room was a cauldron of activity. There were phone calls to relatives, nurses and aides coming and going and papers to be signed confirming the Queen Bee's death. I sat in a daze, still locked to my mother's hand, silently witnessing it all, as though I was gazing in on someone else's dream. I once read in the *Tibetan Book of Living and Dying* that the moments immediately before and after one's death are critical times for the dying person's spirit. I wanted so desperately to help my mother's spirit find a place of beauty and quiet rest. I selfishly wanted to direct her to my rose garden. I needed to know she would always be nearby. All was well in my ethereal world till Bossy Sha barked, "Be ready at noon!" As she left the room, passing by me still clutching my mother's hand, Sha rolled her eyes, shook her head and said, "You are *so* weird!"

Around 9:30 A.M. Aunt Augusta confiscated a hot breakfast plate and brought it to me. I sat and ate the scrambled eggs, sausage and toast. Augusta and I laughed about how it would make the Queen Bee happy to see me eating. Especially meat! But we really laughed when the guy from the mortuary arrived and, wheeling in the gurney, found me talking with eggs in my mouth to my dead mother.

But from that point on, nothing was funny anymore.

It was time to leave. It was time for our final good-byes. There we were, Aunt Augusta and I, hauling away all the old junk and decorations we had brought to cheer up our mother. We packed up everything but we couldn't take that last step out the door. It was as if we stood on the edge of a precipice. We were both crying. I finally took Augusta's hand and made her leave the room with me. We were sobbing loudly. The other residents roaming the lobby in their wheelchairs looked at us terrified. They must have known no one ever left that place alive. I had to hold Augusta up and keep her moving toward the front door. In retrospect, maybe it was Augusta holding me up. We both wanted to run back, but I knew if either of us gave in, we could never leave again.

We were quite a pair. Like Lucy and Ethel having a bad day.

The funeral wasn't as bad as I was afraid it would be. It was in fact beautiful in many ways. We had planned to each place a single, long-stemmed, yellow Peace rose on the casket as it was lowered into the ground. But once we began, we were unable to stop. One after another, we laid gigantic orange and yellow sun-flowers, tall blue delphiniums, Royal Highness pink tea roses and, the Queen Bee's favorite, red and yellow gladiolas on her casket. There we were, my sisters, me and Aunt Fizz among close family and friends. Fizz was praying in Hebrew, saying the names of all of our mother's grieving family members in Israel. For what seemed like a lifetime, we stood there tossing flowers. It felt so right.

It's over now, Jack. I feel as if something has been taken from me that I was not yet prepared to give up. There's a loss and an empti-ness that I can't quite shake. I think about a line the author Mary Gordon once wrote: "Only the silence and emptiness following a moment of forgiveness can stop the monster of deadly anger." I feel the silence and the emptiness.

I think often of how the people in our lives enrich us. How life is about giving, and how much my mother gave me. I think often of the lessons she taught me, and about the strength she saw inside me that I never felt I possessed. I think about my parents, my grandparents and their parents' parents. Among them are found the brave Holocaust survivors who are compelled to never let it happen again. There are those scarred and shamed by domestic abuse, too embattled to ever trust again. And there are those who each day must find the courage and the willingness to forgive. It makes me all the more determined to create change, work toward peace, have faith and be grateful always for all that I have.

On the flight back to San Francisco, I quietly stared out the window while Papa bored you to sleep with another of his Blue

Chips-Chips wilderness stories: "We were camped along the banks of the Amazon Mississippi. . . ." Then he asked me to tell him my favorite memory of my mother. There are so many but one seems to stand above the rest. One balmy August night Aunt Sha was house-sitting for Billy Davis, a music producer, in upstate New York. I was home from college. The Queen Bee and I took the train out of the unbearably humid city to stay for the weekend. While Sha was grilling chicken on the upper terrace, my mother and I were down below at the swimming pool, which was surrounded by trellises of honeysuckle and jasmine vines. I was wearing the skimpy leopard-skin bikini my mother had bought for me in her efforts to make me more feminine, while she was wearing her yellow flowery bathing suit. All day long we had been sunbathing, reading magazines, drinking iced tea, analyzing men—living the good life. At sunset we went swimming. I was in the shallow end of the pool while my mother was paddling around in the deep end. After a few minutes she gracefully pulled off her bathing suit and simply let it float away.

I looked at her in shock and cried out, "Ma, what are you doing?!"

"I'm skinny-dipping!" she replied proudly.

She was having so much fun, I decided to join her. We swam to each other, laughing wildly. I laughed so hard I was sure I would drown. There she was, the Queen Bee, doggy-paddling toward me with her shiny, flamboyant Jackie O. kerchief tied around her face. She was carefree and alive, her glossy, geranium lipstick accentuating a rapturous smile and the scent of her Miss Dior perfume filling the air. We came together in the middle of the iridescent pool where our feet could barely touch the ground. I was laughing so hard I could barely speak. "Ma, you're skinny-dipping! I can't believe it."

With her head tossed back and her face against the fiery sunset sky, she laughed that famous laugh of hers that starts with a loud *phaa* and goes on and on, eyes closed and shoulders shaking. In the midst of splashing and laughing, trying to hold each other up, she looked at me and asked, "What kind of mother is this?!"

About the Author

ANNIE SPIEGELMAN is a First Assistant Director in the Director's Guild of America and the author of *Annie's Garden Journal: Reflections on Roses, Weeds, Men and Life* published in 1996 and listed as a Border's Original Voices selection. She lives in Petaluma, California with her family.

A portion of the proceeds from this book will be donated to the ACT—*Adults and Children Together Against Violence*—project developed by the American Psychological Association and the National Association for the Education of Young Children. The ACT project helps adults to be positive role models and to protect young children from later involvement in violence. To learn more about this important project, visit their website at www.actagainstviolence.org.

against violence